# A USEFUL COMPANION

# A Useful Companion

*A Reader's Commentary on the*
*Tolkien Legendarium*

Donald T. Williams

DeWard
for your journey

# Contents

# Introduction

I first read *The Lord of the Rings* in the summer of 1968, the summer between my junior and senior years of high school. My next official act was immediately to start over and read it again, including every word of the appendices. I could not stand for it to be over! I have read the Trilogy and *The Hobbit* almost every year since. I added the great essays on Beowulf and Fairy Stories and the shorter stories, "Smith of Wooton Major," "Farmer Giles of Ham," and "Leaf by Niggle" the next year and *The Silmarillion* as soon as it came out. It became an annual summer ritual that I used to maintain my tenuous grip on sanity. Once I had started my teaching career, it also served to clean my mind out from all the garbage that had collected in it from all the freshman essays I had graded during the previous school year. Now that I am retired, the ritual is no longer quite so necessary, but it remains every bit as desirable. I have no plans to quit as long as my eyes and brain are still minimally functional. I'm on something like trip number fifty-eight as I type.

I have learned quite a bit in the process about Middle-earth and about our own world. That is not a great boast. Prolonged exposure to the wisdom of Gandalf, the leadership of Aragorn, the integrity of Faramir (the book Faramir, not the Jackson movie one), the commitment of Sam, the self-sacrifice of Frodo, and the faithful friendship of Aragorn, Legolas, and Gimli, and of Frodo, Sam, Merry, and Pippin—if you don't learn anything from that, your learner's broken. Quite a lot of whatever wisdom and insight I have managed to pick up in seven-plus decades of living I owe to Tolkien and his characters. If I am still capable of egregious folly at times, that is not their fault.

Along the way I also absorbed a good share of the secondary literature and even became a bit of a Tolkien scholar myself. I have written quite a lot about the ways in which Tolkien's sub-creation reflects the biblical worldview and how this is an important key to the meaning of the story. Those efforts culminated in the book *An Encouraging Thought*.[1] There I treated that subject, as most treatments do, topically. But my annual readings gave me the idea for a different approach: not topical but episodic.

A couple of years ago I started keeping a journal of my reading, recording some of the insights that my five-plus decades of engagement with Tolkien have brought me. I found myself talking about the meaning of the work, of what Tolkien called its "applicability,"[2] and of its artistry. Those journal entries became the seedbed of this book. The advantage of this approach is that these observations arise organically from the *reading experience* as we start with the creation story of Middle-earth in *The Silmarillion* and move chronologically from there to the birth of the Fourth Age at the end of the Trilogy. So I invite you to come along with me and compare notes as we share the glorious experience of reading the greatest work of fantasy ever composed. My book is organized according to the portion I happen to have read on a given day as the weeks unfolded. That is just a convenience. Your pace isn't likely to correspond with mine, nor does it need

---

[1] Donald T. Williams, *An Encouraging Thought: The Christian Worldview in the Writings of J. R. Tolkien* (Cambridge, OH: Christian Publishing House, 2018). See also *Mere Humanity: Christian Perspectives on the Human from G. K. Chesterton, C. S. Lewis, and J. R. R. Tolkien on the Human Condition*, 2nd ed. (Tampa: DeWard, 2018), "A Far Green Country: The Eschatology of Tolkien's Middle-earth." *Theology and Tolkien: Constructive Theology*, ed. Douglas Estes (NY: Lexington Books/Fortress Academic, 2024): 301–15, etc.

[2] J. R. R. Tolkien, "Foreword," *The Fellowship of the Ring* (NY: Ballantine, 1982): 11.

to. Whenever you reach one of the bits about which I wrote, the commentary will be there waiting for you.

This book assumes that you are already a reader of Tolkien (or at least a fan of the movies) and know the basic outlines of the story. It is *not* an *introduction* to Tolkien. Any readers who tried to use it that way would be frustrated both by spoilers and by constant references to things of which they are ignorant. So if you still need to read Tolkien for the first time, put this book down right now and go do so! I think this book might make an interesting companion, though, for your *second* reading, or any reading subsequent to that. Those like me who love Middle-earth and cannot keep from coming back to it will find, I hope, a "useful companion" for the journey. One recalls that Gandalf employs that phrase to describe Bill the Pony. I hope I don't have as much baggage as Bill did, but I know I am like him in the way the journey has been good for me, and I hope to prove as faithful.

# DAY 1
# "The Ainulindale"

Not quite a decade after I first read *The Lord of the Rings*, the long-awaited prequel came out. *The Silmarillion* is not a finished work. Edited by Tolkien's son Christopher from his father's notes, it is not as well developed or as polished at the Ring trilogy and lacks the anchoring of the high and noble in the recognizably human and earthy world provided by the Hobbits (who are best understood as a sub-species of Mortal Men). It is not the masterpiece that the trilogy is, but those who love Middle-earth value it for its own sake and for the way it fleshes out the hints in the appendices to *The Return of the King* to provide the back story to the Ring cycle. Nevertheless, it does contain "The Ainulindale," the creation story of Middle Earth. And that is one of the most beautiful and profound passages Tolkien ever wrote.

There was Iluvatar, the One, and the Ainur, the children of Iluvatar (roughly corresponding to the biblical angels). Iluvatar sings to them a great theme of music and asks them to form it into a symphony, with each of them, according to his stature, contributing his own notes and elaborations. But Melkor decides to make his own music, a harsh and braying sound not in harmony with the rest. Some of the Ainur join him, while others try to maintain the original melody. There is a great war in heaven between these two versions of the music until Iluvatar introduces a second and a third theme which take up the notes of Melkor and dovetail them back into the work, overcoming the cacophony in a final harmonic resolution. Everyone is standing around, as it were, asking, "What just happened?" And Iluvatar tells them that what they have just heard will be given reality as the history of the world (Ea, the universe, and Arda, Middle-earth within it), so that they may see what they have done. This will demonstrate to all that, contrary to the rebellion of Melkor, Iluvatar *is* Iluvatar and no one can alter the music in his despite.

Some of the Ainur (who become known as the Valar) enter into this new world, Middle-earth, to guide its history in accordance with the music. Melkor thus becomes known as Morgoth, the great Enemy of the First Age of Middle Earth—the Satan figure. Sauron, the super-villain of the Third Age, is a servant of Morgoth. But despite all these Enemies can do of evil, Iluvatar with the aid of the faithful Valar will guide the history of Middle-earth toward the ultimate resolution of the Final Chord.

This sets the stage for everything that follows. For current readers who take the whole *legendarium* in chronological order, it tells them at the outset that Middle-earth is an explicitly theistic world. They are thus prepared to understand that the one who meant Bilbo to find the Ring is most definitely a Person with a name: Eru Iluvatar, the One. It prepares them to understand why that fact is an encouraging thought: It means that Frodo is not left to his own devices and that Gandalf's plan might actually be true wisdom and not the fool's hope it would otherwise seem to be. For the many of us who encountered *The Hobbit* and *The Lord of the Rings* before *The Silmarillion* was available, it turns what were at first only hints of the biblical underpinnings of Tolkien's world into solid signposts.

There is a great deal of controversy amongst Tolkien scholars over whether his world is Christian, pagan, or some mixture of both. There might be some excuse for the Pagan Middle-earth thesis if we had started with "The Valquenta" and did not come to it straight from "The Ainulindale." I submit that "The Ainulindale" is the key to sorting all of that that out. Here we may stand on the Meneltarma, as it were, and see the world with Tolkien's eyes. From this height we can see the Big Picture, and it is not only generically theistic but specifically (though not overtly) biblical. We see that Iluvatar is indeed worthy of all praise as the Source of all that is true, good, and beautiful. We see the price entailed in the creation of significant creatures whose acts make a difference to the world, and hints of how Iluvatar will bear that price himself. And therefore, we see how it is possible to maintain one's faith in Iluvatar and to believe in light and hope despite the darkness that seems to surround us here in our own age of Arda marred. And that is an encouraging vision indeed.

# DAY 2
# "The Valaquenta"

"The Valaquenta" summarizes what we know about the Valar, the Ainur who entered into the history of Ea to guide its unfolding according to the Great Music of "The Ainulindale."

The hasty have read this section and gotten the idea that Middle-earth is polytheistic. But that reading is swiftly contradicted by the text. "The Ainulindale" begins with "There was Eru, the One." "The Valaquenta" begins, "In the beginning there was Eru, the One." The deliberate echo of Genesis should confirm what Eru's reiterated first designation entails: The Valar might look like gods to pagans who do not know any better, but they are more properly parallel to something more like the biblical angels. And Eru is not *a* god; he is God. Middle-earth is a theistic universe.

Why does this matter? One of the bigger controversies amongst interpreters of Tolkien is over the role of the Christian worldview in his fiction. Is Middle-earth essentially Christian, essentially pagan, or is it some kind of synthesis of the two—and if it is a synthesis, is it Christian with pagan coloring or vice versa? The discussion curiously parallels debates over the nature of the Christian influence on *Beowulf.* Despite telling us plainly that Middle-earth is fundamentally Christian, yea, Catholic,[3] Tolkien

---

[3] J. R. R. Tolkien, *The Letters of J. R. R. Tolkien.* Ed. Humphrey Carpenter (Boston: Houghton Mifflin, 1981): 182.

made the debate possible by drawing liberally on both Christian and pagan sources. Outside of Tolkien's Christian readership, it does not look likely to be settled any time soon.

I suggested above that "The Valaquenta," along with "The Ainulindale," is a key to solving this dilemma. "The Ainulindale" makes the theistic nature of Tolkien's world unavoidable. Adding "The Valquenta" demonstrates the fact that, while the Christian worldview is big enough to contain the valid insights of paganism, the pagan worldview is not big enough to return the favor. If there were no One behind the Valar, they would be forced to try to take on roles too big for them, and they would fail. Manwe's vision, which seems prophetic to the Children of Iluvatar, is nonetheless limited by his own limited participation in The Great Music. If he were the mysterious person who will mean for Bilbo to find the Ring and for Frodo to have it, this realization could not contain the encouraging thought Gandalf finds in it. Only Iluvatar can mean or intend such things in ways that do not compromise the freedom of the Children involved, for such a providential involvement requires access to those mysteries that lie in the freedom of Iluvatar and are beyond the capacity of any finite being, even one so powerful as Manwe. "For to none but himself has Iluvatar revealed all that he has in store, and in every age there come forth things that are new and have no forthtelling, for they did not proceed from the past."[4]

By the same token, there is room in the Christian worldview for the stoic pessimism and heroic courage that are presented in Middle-earth and often cited as pagan in their origin and inspiration. The fallenness of the world—that fact that we live in Arda Marred—means that in the short run, particularly in the frame of any single mortal life, ultimate victory over evil is not anticipated.

[4] J. R. R. Tolkien, *The Silmarillion*, ed. Christopher Tolkien (Boston: Houghton Mifflin, 1977): 18.

Therefore, something like Northern Heroic Courage may well be what is called for in the present. But the pagan worldview is not large enough to contain the Christian hope. The gods are *merely* the "powers of the world." They are trapped within the circles of the world and hence limited by the cycles of time even as mortals are. Zeus cannot overturn the fate of Hector, however much he might have wanted to. But because the Valar ultimately serve Iluvatar, they can be His instruments in bringing to light realities from outside the circles of the world, Hence there will be a Final Chord, and hope cometh from the West.

People who want to preserve the "pagan" elements of Tolkien's worldview then are not wholly wrong. But they lack the larger vision that is capable of containing them and giving them a meaning and a role they are not capable of in themselves. The first two sections of the published *Silmarillion* can help us see that larger vision.

# DAY 3
# The Silmarillion
## *Chapters 1–9*

The two Trees, Laurelin and Telperion, whose fruit is golden and silver light, are one of Tolkien's most intriguing images of Arda pristine, of the world as it should have been. Deeply rooted as Yggdrasil and wholesome as the Edenic Tree of Life, their loss introduces us to Middle-earth as we have known it: to Arda marred. Morgoth and Ungoliant's unprovoked destruction of such beauty reveals the gratuitous spitefulness and plain ugliness of evil. But the Trees can yet be saved, for it is their light that the silmarils contain, if only Feanor their maker—the greatest Sub-Creator of the children of Iluvatar—will consent to sacrifice them. He is summoned to the Ring of Doom so the Valar can make that request. And now the real tragedy of Arda marred is about to begin. For his refusal will be a wound that will require a healing of such a depth that not all the Valar together will suffice to achieve it.

When Aule at the Ring of Doom warns the other Valar not to be hasty because they are asking a greater thing of Feanor than they know, what does he mean? We remember from "The Valaquenta" his own willingness to sacrifice his Dwarves if they had been contrary to the will of Iluvatar, and his words are given great weight by that memory. That weight comes from the fact that Aule understands by experience the depths of the connection between the creator and his creation—a profound insight into the character of Iluvatar himself which no other Vala or Elf can quite fully appreciate in the same way. Aule alone then fully understands the cost of the sacrifice being asked of Feanor. The closest parallel in our own history might be Abraham and the profound faith shown by his willingness to sacrifice Isaac. Such was the sacrifice Aule had offered to make himself, though Iluvatar in his grace did not finally require it of him. Reminiscent of Abraham's sacrifice of Isaac, Aule's offer to sacrifice his Dwarves is a paradigmatic moment. It reveals in the offer the kind of sacrificial worship Iluvatar is worthy of and inspires in the faithful. And Iluvatar's gracious refusal of that offer reveals the worthiness of Iluvatar to receive that worship.

Sadly, Feanor does not know any of this. Hence, he loses the opportunity to ponder Aule's wisdom, speaking hastily himself in his passion and refusing the sacrifice that would have restored the Trees.

Would Feanor have needed to break all three of his silmarils to achieve that restoration? Surely, one thinks, two at most, one per Tree, would have sufficed? But nobody stops to ask such questions. This is part of the tragedy. And then we find that Morgoth has stolen the silmarils while they were being debated. Now we are on the road to the Oath of Feanor, the Kin-Slaying of Alqualonde, and the whole sad history of Middle-earth until its final redemption. For now Arda is marred, not just in its physical architecture, but in the very character of the children that Iluvatar had created to inhabit it and complete its beauty.

How is this so? Feanor has chosen to put silmaril and self above the will of Iluvatar and the good of Arda. To be precise, he has chosen, in Tolkien's terms used elsewhere, to treat his sub-creation as if it were primary Creation. (If you have not read Tolkien's essay "On Fairie Stories,"[5] you might want to do so and then skip ahead to those chapters of this book to fully understand this point and its importance to Tolkien's worldview.) This is essentially idolatry. We are meant to understand the depths of the temptation, the severity of the trial. We are also meant to see that once Feanor has made that choice, the supreme wickedness of the Kinslaying is inevitable. It is *contained* in the idolatry, entailed by it. How? Once we put the self in the place of God, nothing else can remain sacred, not even the lives of our fellow creatures.

Suddenly, Treebeard's words about "hastiness," still ages in the future, take on a new meaning and a new weight.

We are in for a rough ride. Morgoth will torture and ruin captive Elves into the Orcs because evil can only corrupt a good that already exists; it cannot truly create. And this is said to be his greatest evil, worse even by implication than the destruction of the Trees, because of what it does directly to children of Iluvatar (never mind the immeasurable destruction the Orcs will wreak in coming ages).[6] But we remember the Final Chord and so are granted the faith to believe that at its end is Eucatastrophe. But that end may be a long way off as mortal Man—or even Elf—counts the passage of time. And no amount of hastiness will now serve to shorten it.

---

[5] J. R. R. Tolkien, "On Fairie Stories," *The Tolkien Reader* (NY: Ballantine, 1966): 2–73.
[6] *Silmarillion*, op. cit., 50.

# DAY 4
# The Silmarillion
## *Chapterts 11–13*

I stopped today at the death of Feanor. So much death, and it is not going to end any time soon,

Speaking of death, the most interesting part of this section is the coming of Mortal Men. The name of that species is not just a fortuitously sonorous alliteration; their mortality is the most significant thing about them. Unlike the Elves, who experience immortality within the life of the world, Mortal Men die and leave the world indeed. Is it the Gift of Men or the Doom of Men? Is it a blessing or a punishment? Yes. It will eventually be revealed as both. But as yet, nobody seems to have a clear notion of what that means.

Given that the Translator of *The Red Book of Westmarch* into modern English was a certified human being, one would think Tolkien would have some insight into his own species; but Man is the most mysterious creature in Middle-earth, no less so to himself than to Dwarf, Elf, or Vala. Because he came in with the Third Theme of Iluvatar and was not otherwise revealed in the Music, Man is uniquely opaque even to the far-seeing Valar. Their memories of their own contributions to the Music give them no insight into him, though those memories are as fate to all things else. Man's very limitation entails a freedom unique among the children of Iluvatar. Is he truly free? It's complicated. Answers of yes and no both seem to be required. Enslaved by sin and his own passions since his fall, he can still make choices that change the course of history, that change the world. His mortality as explained by Tolkien is a wonderful symbol for Man's unique ability to surprise with unexpected moves that can remake the world and affect its very history. That freedom remains a mystery for all that.

This mystery all the true sages confess. Justly did Pope describe Man as

> Placed on this isthmus of a middle state,
> A being darkly wise and rudely great:
> With too much knowledge for the Skeptic side,
> With too much weakness for the Stoic's pride,
> He hangs between; in doubt to act, or rest,
> In doubt to deem himself a God, or Beast;
> In doubt his Mind or Body to prefer,
> Born but to die, and reas'ning but to err;
> Alike in ignorance, his reason such,
> Whether he thinks too little or too much:
> Chaos of Thought and Passion all confused;
> Still by himself abused or disabused;
> Created half to rise and half to fall;
> Great lord of all things, yet a prey to all;
> Sole judge of Truth, in endless Error hurled:
> The glory, jest, and riddle of the world.[7]

The only reason we are given for this is the Third Theme and the redemption of Arda. It is somehow connected to Man's mortality. Looking back from the standpoint of later revelation and

---

[7] Alexander Pope, "Essay on Man," *The Poems of Alexander Pope*, ed. John Butt (New Haven, CT: Yale Univ. Pr., 1963): 516.

its developed theology, we can connect it also to his creation in the *imago Dei* and his role as a sub-creator.

Hmmm. Maybe our Translator understands this mystery about as well as any mortal can after all!

# DAY 5

# The Silmarillion

## *Chapters 14–15*

Thingol has just learned the truth about the Kin-Slaying from Finrod and Angrod, and in response bans the Noldoran tongue in his realm of Doriath. The original language of the Noldor thus becomes a kind of Elf-Latin, a language of lore only, henceforth. For Tolkien the philologist, this would be not the least tragedy flowing from the hubris of Feanor.

What is a philologist? What is philology? We are familiar with philosophy as the combination of two Greek words: *philos*, love, and *sophia*, wisdom. So philosophy is (or is supposed to be) the love of wisdom. Philology is *philos* plus *logos*, the love of words. It is that branch of scholarship where linguistics and literature meet. It studies the history of words and of language the better to understand their use in ancient literature; it studies literature that is old enough to need that kind of elucidation from the standpoint of its language as situated in that history. We meet the word most often (outside of Tolkien's biography) as allied to the two most popular fields of literature where its help is needed: Classical Philology and Biblical Philology.

Tolkien was by all accounts the greatest philologist of his generation, the world's foremost authority on the medieval dialects of the English West Midlands. He used this expertise professionally as Professor of Anglo-Saxon and as the editor and one of the better translators of the Gawain Poet, a contemporary of Chaucer whose Middle English is much more difficult for modern readers because, unlike Chaucer's, it was not in the dialect that was the direct ancestor of their own modern English.[8] But Tolkien's most signal and profound use of that expertise was in the composition of his legendarium.

One of the most important things to know about Middle-earth is that it had its origin in the youthful Tolkien's desire to create a language with its own unique vocabulary and grammar. That language was Elvish and its descendants. Tolkien realized that for his language truly to feel real to him, it needed a people to speak it, Then that people needed a world to live in—and they needed a history, along with other peoples to whose speech theirs could be related. How else could their speech have cognates and etymologies—just like a real language? And that is how we got Middle-earth. This tells us why Tolkien's names are so good; it also tells us why his imaginary world feels so real. As with the primary world, so with Tolkien's Middle-earth: In the beginning was the Word. It also helps us begin to see something of what it must have meant to him to have even the languages of Middle-earth impacted by the curse. Loss of language is a loss of culture greater than which none can hardly be conceived.

Meanwhile, elsewhere among the exiles, we have a foreshadowing whose significance cannot be overestimated. Turgon has finished Gondolin but not yet inhabited it. Ulmo gives him a profound bit of advice: "Love not too well the work of thy hands," for ultimately hope comes only from the West.[9]

---

[8] J. R. R. Tolkien and E. V. Gordon, eds., *Sir Gawain and the Green Knight*, 1925; 2nd edition ed. Norman Davis (Oxford: The Clarendon Press, 1967), and J. R. R. Tolkien, trans., *Sir Gawain and the Green Knight, Pearl, and Sir Orfeo* (Boston, MA: Houghton Mifflin, 1975).

[9] *Silmarillion*, op. cit., 125.

This is what Feanor should have remembered. The glory of the children of Iluvatar is that they are real creators—but they need to remember that they are sub-creators. (Again: If you have not read Tolkien's essay "On Fairie Stories," you might want to do so and then skip to those chapters of this book at this point.) We can add real elaborations to the beauties of Arda, but they are derivative, dependent on Iluvatar's original propounding of the themes of the Great Music. To refuse to make our elaborations is to refuse our own significance. But to treat them as ultimate, to put them before the will of Iluvatar or the good of Arda, to act as if *they* are the primary themes, is to be guilty of the sin of Morgoth. It is a form of idolatry.

This idolatry, this failure to love the work of his own hands *appropriately*, is the source of Feanor's fall. It is a supreme irony that by cursing Morgoth and insisting on opposing him on his own terms, Feanor becomes enmeshed in the very fall from grace that Morgoth represents. He makes his silmarils his ultimate value. This is a powerfully corrupting choice. It is no accident then that the Oath leads quickly to the Kinslaying. To love the work of my own hands in the wrong way is to love it more than the life of my neighbor. It is to insist on singing my own notes irrespective of how they impact the rest of the Music. Yes. This is what Feanor should have remembered. And it is what we should remember.

So Ulmo's warning is the whole history of Middle-earth, including our own Fourth Age, compounded into one sentence. "Love not too well the work of thy hands." Our incapacity to remember this truth lies behind all our own still growing entanglement in evil. But the Third Theme has been introduced, and the Final Chord is yet to be sung. Even so, come …

# DAY 6
# The Silmarillion
## *Chapters 16–18*

After hearing about them earlier, we finally meet mortal Men. "A darkness lies behind us," Beor said, "and we have turned our backs upon it and we do not desire to return thither even in our thoughts."[10] And that is all he will say.

What is this darkness, and why won't Beor talk about it? Clyde S. Kilby said that, when he was living with Tolkien and helping him to organize his notes toward the completion of *The Silmarillion*, Tolkien described to him his problem in depicting the fall of mankind near the beginning of the story. "'How far we have fallen!' he exclaimed—so far, he felt, that it would seem impossible ever to find an adequate prototype or to imagine the contrast between Eden and the disaster that followed."[11] From which we can gather that something like the biblical story must lie behind Beor's words. They are Tolkien's way of expressing the difficulty of the description and the depth of the disaster. And that may be the most that can be said until biblical revelation provides more insight in the book of Genesis, sometime after the Third Age.

---

[10] Ibid., 141.

[11] Clyde S. Kilby, *Tolkien and* The Silmarillion: *A Glimpse of the Man and his World* (Wheaton, IL: Harold Shaw, 1976): 59.

Meanwhile, Feanor's sons continue to love too well the work of their hands, and the Exiles who follow them are entangled in the effects of this idolatry. They forfeit the blessing of the Valar and come at times to resemble Morgoth even in their fierce and undying opposition to him. They are reduced to being his rivals in the lust for the silmarils, a lust that is similar in its nature as well as in its object. Thus the fall of the Eldar is both like and unlike the fall of Msn. It is similar in the lusts it engenders and in their source and their effects. Yet, as profound as their fall is, the Elves do not seem to have fallen *as a race*, and their essential character is not compromised in the same way as Men's was by their fall. Feanor was not the father of all Elfdom, nor its head, as Adam was for Mankind. (See Romans chapter 5.) An Elf who remains faithful or who repents can be therefore untainted by evil in a way that no mortal man in this life can quite match, as characters like Elrond and Galadriel will show us when we get to *The Lord of the Rings*. Still, mortals like an Aragorn or a Faramir can manifest a real and impressive integrity by what we know from later theology to be grace. Such an achievement is not to be discounted, but it is to be marveled at.

In summary, the Elves' original sin was like ours in its ties to idolatry and its devastating effects on the history of Arda, but unlike ours in the way it affects the Elves as a race. And what was ours? In keeping with his history of Middle-earth in an age even prior to that of the Old Testament, Tolkien will do nothing more than to hint at it.

But the effects are indeed devastating. Dagor Bragollach wreaks havoc, and Fingolfin falls. "The Noldor did not yet comprehend the fullness of the power of Morgoth, nor understand that unaided war against him was without final hope."[12] It's not as if Manwe,

---

[12] *Silmarillion*, op. cit., 150.

Mandos, and Ulmo have not tried to tell them. Hope comes only from the West. And in the primary world there is no other name under Heaven whereby we must be saved. The Fourth Age does not listen any better than the first three did, it would seem.

# DAY 7

# The Silmarillion

## *Chapter 19: Beren and Luthien*

The tale of Beren and Luthien is the high point of *The Silmarillion*. The tale is powerfully beautiful, and a little knowledge of its background only enhances its poignance.

It is nothing less than heart-stopping, for example, to realize that the whole chapter is a love song to Tolkien's wife, Edith. For while he certainly never claimed to be Beren, he was very clear that Edith was Luthien. He had the name carved on her tombstone and wrote to his son Christopher that "Mummy … was (and knew she was) my *Luthien*."[13] He went on to say, "I never called Edith *Luthien*—but she was the source of the story that in time became the chief part of *The Silmarillion*. It was first conceived in a small woodland glade filled with hemlocks at Roos in Yorkshire."[14]

There is nothing specifically autobiographical about the story beyond the fact that the young Edith had raven hair and was a singer and a dancer. But if you could have asked Tolkien what she meant to him (in the letter he even imagines a potential biographer doing so), the tale of Beren and Luthien would have been his answer. I don't suppose any deeper compliment has been paid

---

[13] Tolkien, *Letters*, op. cit., 120.
[14] Ibid.

to any lover since Dante fulfilled his vow to write about Beatrice what had never been written about any woman.[15] But for Tolkien, it was no romanticized nostalgia for an idealized figure of youthful memory. He wrote those words to Christoper at the end of a full lifetime of marriage not devoid of struggles.

This then may be the most intensely personal chapter of the whole legendarium. Whether Edith ever read it, or what she thought about it, we do not and should not know. We must draw an appropriate curtain of privacy over that information and be content with the glimpse we have been given.

Beren son of Barahir is a grim mortal Man pursued by the servants of Morgoth. Luthien the Elf maiden, daughter of Melian and Thingol, is the most beautiful of all the children of Iluvatar. They meet and fall in love. But Thingol will only give his daughter's hand in marriage to this mortal if he brings him a silmaril from the crown of Morgoth. Thingol thinks he has gotten rid of Beren, cleverly condemned him to death. But, driven by love, Luthien flees to be with him and through the great power of her magic they achieve that impossible quest, though at great price. The impact of the recovered jewel on the Elf kingdoms and the union of Elves and Men in Beren and Luthien become the forces that drive the Silmarillion to its resolution, for of their line come Earendil and the very Elrond Halfelven who will play a pivotal role in the Second and Third Ages.

For now, we leave those threads to play themselves out in subsequent chapters and note the way Tolkien uses a creative transformation of the Orpheus myth to give the story of Beren and Luthien much of the power it has in itself. Orpheus's song came painfully close to recovering his beloved wife Eurydice from

---

[15] Dante Alighiere, *Vita Nuova: Italian Text with Facing English Translation*, trans. Dino S. Cervigni and Edward Vasta (Notre Dame, IN: Univ. of Notre Dame Pr., 1995): 144–5; cf. Dante Alighiere, *The Divine Comedy 1: Hell*, trans. Dorothy L. Sayers (1300; Baltimore: Penguin, 1949): 27–8.

death, its evocation of the sorrow of the human condition forcing a momentary tear of molten iron even from the implacable eye of Hades (the most hated of all the immortals, as Homer tells us, because he is the only god who never answers prayer). Fate ironically prevents the fulfillment of the conditions Hades had imposed so that Eurydice is lost again at the very threshold of the achievement of new life. Orpheus is not to look back as Eurydice follows him back to the world of light until they have fully emerged from the cavern—but when she stumbles and falls, he turns one step too soon to catch her and break her fall, only to lose her a second time even more heartbreaking than the first. But that is the moment that lets Orpheus's evocation of human grief have the same effect on us that it had on Hades.

In Tolkien's adaptation, it is the woman who sings, not to evoke compassion from Morgoth (there is none to be evoked) but to overpower his evil and send him to sleep, allowing Beren to cut the Silmaril from his crown. But Luthien's greatest artistry is reserved for Mandos. To him she sings all the sorrows of both Elves and Men in the most beautiful song ever sung, with the result that she wins from Mandos a brief reprieve from death for herself and Beren at the price of surrendering her immortality, along with the doom that their descendants will have the choice of which kindred they will belong to—a doom that will still be impacting the fate of Middle-earth two ages later in the person of Arwen Undomiel.

The power of love, the power of art, and the mysterious and surprising connection between beauty and sorrow are themes Tolkien will keep coming back to. Their roots are here, in the tale we may believe was the closest to Tolkien's own heart.

# DAY 8
# The Silmarillion
## *Chapter 20*

Things continue to go from bad to worse. Even the brief happiness of Beren and Luthien comes at a terrible price.

The two deaths I mourn the most are Finrod Felagund and Beleg Strongbow. Even splendid characters like them who are faithful to the end are caught up in the curse that flows from Feanor's idolatry. Nothing in Middle-earth can escape it. Later Elrond and Galadriel may be able to use their elven Rings to create a respite from it. But this respite they can only maintain for a while. Their little realms will still be part of Middle-earth, if not fully integrated with its time. They are not the West—only hints and reminders that point to it. And they are fated to fade very quickly once the Fourth Age begins. Let us imagine Lorien as it might have been after the last of its people had gone West over the sea:

**Loth Lorien**
From silver trunk the golden leaf
Blows through the old abandoned fief,
For Time, the robber and the thief,
Has brought the hidden realm to grief:
The wonder is withdrawn.

Now far beyond the Western Sea
The merry folk have gone to be
Naught but a fading memory
    In Caras Galadon.

For untold years Galadriel
Did weave her magic and her spell.
Nor warg nor orc nor dragon fell
Could enter the enchanted veil
Until it was withdrawn.
Now in the once protected Wood
The Evil mingles with the Good—
Foul things that never could have stood
    In Caras Galadon.

Now through the hushed and chilling air
There rings no voice of minstrel fair,
No melody of sweetness rare,
No magic words beyond compare;
The music is withdrawn.
The happy sound of harper's glee
Sounds only far beyond the Sea.
The rasping raven's symphony
    Fills Caras Galadon.

In Cerin Amroth, Arwen's tomb
Lies hidden in the gathering gloom.
The niphredil no longer bloom.
She sleeps within that narrow room,
All memory withdrawn.
The sons to Aragorn she bore:
They come to mourn her there no more.
They sleep beneath the marble floor
Of cold and deep Rath Dinen, far
    From Caras Galadon.

A lonely wanderer passes by;
He sees there is no shelter nigh.
The stars are twinkling in the sky.
He groans, and on the ground doth lie
Within his cloak withdrawn.
The leaves are rustling on high.
It seems to him they softly sigh
A sad lament—he know not why—
      In Caras Galadon.[16]

I wonder if the memory of the silmaril's effect on Thingol helped Gandalf and Galadriel to resist the Ring so adamantly in a later age. Galadriel was an eye-witness to the way Thingol's greed awakened by the stone led to the destruction of Doriath. Gandalf as a Maia would have learned about it before being sent from across the sea early in the Third Age. So, presumably, would Saruman. One of them paid better attention than the other.

The greatest faithfulness, of Finrod, Beleg, Galadriel, or even Gandalf, cannot change the fact that we live in Arda marred or keep life in Arda marred from being tragic in the foreseeable future. But it can lead to deeds worthy of song, and they may be rewarded in the Halls of Mandos or (for Mortal Men) beyond the circles of the world. Faith is the ability to believe that such deeds are not wholly in vain. To be amongst the faithful, we no less than they must walk by faith and not by sight (2 Cor 5.7).

---

[16] Donald T. Williams, *Stars through the Clouds: The Collected Poetry of Donald T. Williams*, 2nd ed. (Lynchburg: Lantern Hollow Press, 2020): 356–7.

# DAY 9

# The Silmarillion

## *Chapter 21: Turin*

"For never was there story of more woe / Than this of Juliet and her Romeo."

Thus spake Shakespeare of Stratford and London, ca. 1600—because he had not read "The Tale of Turin Turambar."

And that (almost) is all I am going to have to say about that.

If we are going to take the marring of Arda seriously, and if we understand that it comes from a source as momentous as the abuse of created wills in rebellion against their good Creator, that is, the choice to prefer our own wills embodied in the work of our hands over the will of Iluvatar and the good of His creation, then we must be prepared for there to be episodes of darkness as unremittent and unrelenting as this.

It is made even darker by the fact that there was nothing Turin, Morwen, or Nienor had done *specifically* and *personally* to deserve the particularly twisted and cruelly ironic fate in which they are ensnared. That is how evil the wickedness of Morgoth is. Glaurung is the personification of it. Once you choose your own raucous noise over the Symphony and are even willing to profane the Symphony by insisting on inserting it; once you choose the work of your hands over the good of Arda (for they are one and the same choice), this is the kind of thing you unleash upon the world. It cannot be kept within bounds. The (relative) innocence of its potential victims is no protection for them. All of this is there in that first deliberately discordant note. Do not let Morgoth or his later servants deceive you by calling it artistic license or freedom of expression. Its end is *Turin Turambar turum ambartanen*: "Master of doom by doon mastered."[17] Its end is that fate multiplied in countless ways, not all of which are so stark or so clear, but all of which partake in the reality of Arda marred.

That is how evil the wickedness of Morgoth is. Tolkien was willing to look this evil in the face. He did not blink. Indeed, if your nose is not sufficiently rubbed in it by the chapter in *The Silmarillion*, there is a book-length version available. For me, the chapter is quite enough. I do not regret the chapter or the book, for they are a word in the history of Arda marred. And they are a necessary word.

But they are not the last word.

[17] *Silmarillion*, op. cit., 223.

# DAY 10
# The Silmarillion
## *Chapters 22–24*

Now *The Silmarillion* hastens on to its end, in which the evil forces set in motion by Feanor come to their fulfillment in vast and irremediable destruction of much that is good and fair, yet a destruction that cannot prevent a twinkling light of hope glimmering from the West as Earendil and the surviving silmaril sail across the sky.

Lust corrupts the heart, and pride goeth before a fall. And ever those twin fountains of evil are found working hand in hand. The Nauglamir set with the silmaril leads to the downfall of Doriath. Not all his long life with Melian can prevent Thingol's lust from fueling his pride. So he needlessly insults and tries to cheat the Dwarves who have labored on the necklace, leading to his death. The Dwarves' lust for ancient heirloom and wrought stone is not wholly out of character, but Thingol? Like Solomon at the end of his life, he shows that even the Wise can fall into great folly through lust and pride.

Then Turgon becomes the next tragic figure to love too well the work of his own hands. He is unwilling to part with Gondolin, and so his own pride leads him to refuse the warning and summons of Ulmo, leading to the destruction of his city and his people. In the Third Age, Aragorn will tell Pippin that a man who cannot cast away a treasure at need is in fetters, as even that fool of a Took makes a better choice with his Broach of Lorien. Thus a small virtue is paralleled with a great evil, and the king of men has the perfect commentary on both.

The resolution of *The Silmarillion* through the mission of Earendil seems satisfying and appropriate to me up to a point, but a question remains. "Only one speaking in person for the cause of both Elves and Men, pleading for pardon on their misdeeds and pity on their woes" could move the Valar to relent from their curse and ban.[18] But how does Earendil know that he speaks for all of these people? Nobody has appointed Earendil to speak for them—he just takes it on himself. Are they to be forgiven whether repentant or not? And many (indeed, most) of them are not repentant—either still rebellious or simply not having faced the issue in any clear way. It is a question that puzzles me, but I think that the records of the period are so spotty that we simply don't have enough information to answer it.

What we do know is that the love of Beren and Luthien has literally sowed the seeds of redemption. And we know that, while Morgoth is defeated and banished, his lies and their agents (like Sauron) remain and will have to be dealt with "even unto the latest days."[19] "This was of old the fate of Arda Marred," and if there is any un-marring ahead of us, the Valar may know (in fact they do, because they were there at the Great Music), but they have not revealed it to Elves or Men. Not clearly—not in *The Silmarillion*. But in other texts there are hints.

There are hints indeed. But the ultimate answer lies in the character of Iluvatar and comes from the West. And that is why a figure like Gandalf, a Maia who serves the Secret Fire, is able to

---

[18] *Silmarillion*, op, cit., 244.
[19] Ibid., 255.

be a source of Hope. And it is why Aragorn, who is named Estel ("Hope"), is the embodiment of that hope. But the fruition of all of that is still an age or two away.

Meanwhile, the tragedy of Arda marred continues. We have seen its impact on the Elves. Now we turn to mortal men and must deal with the downfall of Numenor.

# DAY 11

# Akallabeth

The story of Numenor is the story of mankind: goodness and nobility destroyed by complacency and pride, character traits easily twisted into positive evil. In the biblical story it is the lies of Satan, who destroyed his own happiness by refusing to be content to be what he was (a creature), and who could not be content until he had sowed the same discontent into the race of men. In Tolkien's Middle-earth it is the lies of Morgoth spread by his servant, Sauron. Morgoth had not been content to be a musician faithful to the score. He insisted on playing his own notes even if it ruined the Symphony. Their earlier fall (see Day 6) leaves the most noble of mortal men susceptible to his lies, which lead them to be discontent with an immortality that they must now seek beyond the circles of the world.

The story of the Akallabeth then reveals something crucial about the nature and identity of mortal men. Elves were made for immortality within the circles of the world, while Men must find theirs beyond them. That is why the chief characteristic distinguishing Men from Elves is their "seeking elsewhither."[20] Elsewhither: beyond the circles of the world. This characteristic is coordinated with the necessity that men, if they are to be faithful, must, in the biblical phrase "walk by faith and not by sight" (2 Cor

---

[20] J. R. R. Tolkien, *Unfinished Tales*, ed. Christopher Tolkien (Boston: Houghton Mifflin, 1980): 225.

5.7). Tolkien does not cite that passage, though the complaint of the Numenoreans to the messengers of the Valar perhaps echoes it: "Of us is required a blind trust and a hope without assurance, knowing not what lies before us in a little while."[21] Tolkien does not quote the biblical passage, but his Numenoreans are a profound commentary on it. The Apostle Paul is speaking of precisely the form of immortality human beings are offered in the intermediate state before the Resurrection: to be "absent from the body but present with the Lord." To avoid despair, they must believe in a life that by definition they cannot see. Ar Pharazon insists on an immortality that he *can* see, like that of the Elves. He thus betrays not only his obedience to Iluvatar as mediated through the Valar, but the very essence of what it is to be human.

Ar Pharazon insists on getting his immortality here and now, like the Elves—that is, he insists on being allowed to walk by sight and not by faith. So all but a faithful remnant forsake Iluvatar and eventually rebel against their own nature, transgressing the Ban of the Valar. And Numenor, that favored land of favored people, sinks forever beneath the waves and is lost … most appropriately … to sight.

Only Tolkien could capture the full seriousness of Numenor's rebellion and the choices it forced on the faithful. I can only shake my head at it, as in this Clerihew:

**The Fall of Nuumenor**
*A Clerihew*

Ar Pharazon the Golden
Was due quite a scoldin'.
His trip into the West
Was not exactly for the best.[22]

---

[21] *Silmarillion*, op. cit., 265.
[22] Williams, *Stars*, op. cit., 281.

Or, as Tolkien said it better:

Tall ships and tall kings,
Three times three:
What brought they from the foundered land,
O'er the flowing sea?
Seven stars and seven stones
And one white tree.[23]

Ever is pride the downfall of Elves and Men; and ever is there a small number of the Faithful who care more about their people than themselves, more about their integrity than their ego, more about what is right than what is advantageous, more about the meaning of life than its length: people like Aragorn and Faramir in the Third Age and surely some that we can find even now in the Fourth.

It has not changed from of old. Follow Amandil's command—to the East and to exile! That is all.

[23] J. T. R. Tolkien, *The Two Towers* (1954; N.Y.: Ballantine, 1982): 239.

# DAY 12

# "The Rings of Power and the Third Age"

This is the narrative version of the "Tale of Years" from the *The Lord of the Rings* appendices. Not much needs to be said about it, as its insights are covered elsewhere as they occur in the main narrative. It is useful to have the overview both ways. Takeaway: What was intended in another world (long, long ago and far, far away) as a speech of intimidation by Evil will serve here as a salutary warning for the Good [begin Darth Vader voice]: "Do not underestimate the power of the Dark Side."

Yeah, we are still underestimating it in the Fourth Age.

Sigh

# DAY 13
# The Hobbit
## *"An Unexpected Party"*

Reading the core canonical texts in chronological order, as I have done most years, brings you straight from the most daunting material in The Red Book (*The Silmarillion*) to the most engaging and accessible (*The Hobbit*). *The Hobbit* is one of those books, like *The Chronicles of Narnia* or *The Wind in the Willows*, that you can enjoy with profit as a child and come back to as an adult with even greater profit. Then we finish, perfectly, with *The Lord of the Rings*, a work of fully adult fiction that boasts themes as deep and daunting as *The Silmarillion* couched in a narrative as accessible and engaging as *The Hobbit*. No wonder many consider it the greatest work of fiction (not just fantasy) ever composed. (Well, if we can bring ourselves to call it fiction, and not history …) It was deservedly, in three different polls heading into the new millennium, "The Book of the Century."

For now: *The Hobbit*.

Tolkien is really good at opening chapters. "The Ainulindale" in *The Silmarillion*, for example, has some of his most beautiful prose and profound thoughts. And in those opening chapters he is really good at opening lines "In a hole in the ground there lived a hobbit."[24] "When Mr. Bilbo Baggins of Bag End announced that

---
[24] J. R. R. Tolkien, *The Hobbit, or There and Back Again* (1937; NY: Ballantine, 1965): 1.

he would shortly be celebrating his eleventy-first birthday...."[25] As those chapters develop, there is hardly a word out of place.

Here in *The Hobbit*, what would in a lesser writer be a mere infodump keeps you on the edge of your seat as the back story of the Dwarves comes out to the tune of Bilbo's escaping shriek. And the way character is revealed by dialog is unsurpassed. This thankfully includes poetry and song: "Far over the Misty Mountains cold / Through dungeons deep and caverns old ..."[26] That song is one of the things Peter Jackson got right in his movie version of *The Hobbit*. If there were Dwarves and they could sing, they would definitely sing like that. The text of the poem all by itself shows us a passionate people deeply in love with craftsmanship and possessed of very long memories, especially of injustice to which they have been subject.

Character development happens in conversation, too. "Adventures. Nasty, uncomfortable, disturbing things. Make you late for dinner."[27] Fortunately, Bilbo turns out to be neither so prosy nor so sedentary as he likes to think. But for now, he is echoing the limited vision of his neighbors. Well, that is going to change, and we shall see whether Bilbo gains anything by the change.

Then there is Gandalf. "What a lot of things you do use *Good morning* for!"[28] We don't need to see any of his magic or even his famous fireworks to know that his vision pierces beneath the surface. Like his creator, Tolkien, he is finely attuned to words and their meanings. He will use them to prod you into helping with his adventurous plans for the good of Middle-earth of your own free will, a will you did not even realize you had, and he will have fun doing it. Better not try to put anything over on him!

---

[25] J. R. R. Tolkien, *The Fellowship of the Ring*, op. cit., 41.

[26] *The Hobbit*, op. cit., 13.

[27] Ibid., 4.

[28] Ibid., 5.

Yes, this book is going to be every bit as good as it was the last fifty-seven years.

# DAY 14

# The Hobbit

## *"Roast Mutton"*

Trolls is the first adventure? I did not even realize that Middle-earth had Internet, much less Facebook, in the Third Age.

Seriously, the Trolls help to orient us in the Fairy Story (if Wizards, Dwarves and Dragons had not already done so). This means that the longing, the consolation, the eucatastrophe discussed in the essay "On Fairie Stories" (see our chapters on that essay) are all on the table. This is also going to be a world that contains real good and real evil. The dragon is real and evil, but he is far away and legendary and can be dealt with if and when we ever get there. The clumsy and oafish vulgarity that frames the Trolls' real evil (they eat people as well as sheep, after all) serves notice that this is not a picnic and is a table-setter for more serious forms of evil to follow.

Indeed, after many readings one notices all the foreshadowing leading up to the encounter with the trolls in this chapter of those future difficulties that we will encounter later in the story. The provision for funeral expenses in the contract might strike us merely as humorous hyperbole on our first reading. It is that, but there is a serious side to it, too. The bad weather warns us that adventures are not just pony rides in May sunshine, and the loss of the one pony's load of food in the river reminds us that they are not just a series of picnics in the parklike rural landscape of the Shire. All this plus the temptation of the fire seen in the distance through the trees, which won't turn out to be what we hoped, will come to painful fruition in Mirkwood.

Then when we get to Mirkwood, Bilbo's botched burgling of the Trolls and the group's last-minute rescue by Gandalf will give way to Gandalf being away on other business and Bilbo stepping up to find both a courage and a resourcefulness he had never shown before in dealing with Spider and Elf. The parallels with those later events bring out the differences between them and thus highlight the real growth of Bilbo into the Hobbit Gandalf had seen beneath his prosaic surface all along. And that growth is a necessary prelude to the even greater growth required if Bilbo is to deal with the Dragon and the Five Armies. From not understanding how he had managed to get himself pushed out the door of Bag End by Gandalf without a pocket handkerchief to the bold and sacrificial proactive initiative he would show with the Arkenstone: This is a growth arc so impressive that it might seem incredible had it not been prepared for in ways that make it seem inevitable. We believe it partly because turning the unexpected into the inevitable is the genius of the storyteller. And the greatest genius ever to put hand to pen is at work here.

Right now, we are just setting the stage, and setting it for an epic Adventure indeed. One thing is certain: If ponies' saddles had seat belts, it would be time to fasten them.

# DAY 15

# The Hobbit

## *"A Short Rest"*

The visit to Rivendell is a part of this book that I can never quite get past unruffled. Elrond and Rivendell itself are fine, yea, very good ... but who kidnapped all the rest of the Elves and replaced them with silly people from Monty Python? "Tra la la lally here down in the valley"?[29] Seriously? Every other song in both works is perfectly appropriate to the people who sing it. Not this one. (In fairness, Elrond's people will redeem themselves with "Sing all ye joyful"[30] in "The Last Stage.") Granting the shift from children's book to adult fantasy, everything else that makes it into *The Lord of the Rings* from *The Hobbit* is recognizable as itself. Orcs instead of Goblins, fine; they are still believably the same species. Gimli is very believable as the son of Gloin. But these Elves (other than Elrond himself)? No. Eldar they are not.

One forgets this minor irritation however in the wonder of the place itself and the importance of what is revealed there. Rivendell is one of those many places, like Bag End or The Prancing Pony or Bombadil's House or Loth Lorien or Fangorn Forest or Meduseld or Minas Tirith, that are so wonderfully realized and essential to the unfolding of the story that they almost become

---

[29] Ibid., 48.
[30] Ibid., 297.

characters in their own right. We won't feel it fully until we visit in the Trilogy, but already Elrond's house is "perfect whether you like food, or sleep, or work, or story-telling, or singing, or just sitting and thinking best, or a pleasant mixture of them all."[31] Have you known such a place, or even one that hints at being so? To find it is to find the home you never knew you were missing. I have heard that L'Abri was such a place for many when the Schaeffers were there. I think of Snow Wolf Lodge or Tarryall River Ranch in the Colorado Rockies when Summit Gap Year is in residence. This is why real lovers of Middle-earth just want to be there. Give me a seat in the Hall of Fire or a pint to nurse in the Common Room of the Prancing Pony, and I am content. Nothing needs to happen. But, then, wonderful things do happen. It is a compelling combination.

What happens in Rivendell this time is Elrond discovering the Moon Letters on Thorin's map. Magic letters that can only be seen when the same Moon shines behind them as when they were written—and their content is almost as cryptic when read as when it was hidden. "Stand by the grey stone when the thrush knocks, and the setting sun with the last light of Durin's Day will shine upon the keyhole." And Durin's Day is an even rarer meteorological phenomenon; who knows when it will come again? But things in Middle-earth happen for a reason, and luck—if luck you call it—will be with them in the person of Bilbo when the time comes.

After all these readings, I only just realized that Glamdring was Turgon's sword from *The Silmarillion*. Cool. How it got into the Troll's hoard would be a great bit of fan fiction for somebody to write.

---

[31] FOTR, op. cit., 272.

# The Hobbit

### *"Over Hill and Under Hill" and*
### *"Riddles in the Dark"*

In "Over Hill and Under Hill," we see Goblins (Orcs) up close for the first time. They take the evil we saw in the Trolls and turn it up a notch. Colder forms of evil (Smaug, Sauron) more pitiful forms (Gollum) and more insidious forms that hit close to home (Thorin in the grip of his greed, Denethor) are yet to come.

No doubt they are called Goblins, even though Tolkien had already called them Orcs in the yet unpublished *Silmarillion* material, because he was introducing his Middle-earth mythology in a children's book, and children would not doubt have been puzzled by Orcs but would recognize Goblins right off as evil and monstrous, and that would be enough for them to go on with. If you started chronologically with the Silmarillion you will know, as the original readers did not, that they are descended from Elves captured, tortured, corrupted, and ruined by Morgoth or later Sauron. Morgoth and Sauron had to do this because, being evil, they were incapable of true creation, even sub-creation, and could only corrupt something good created by Iluvatar.

Tolkien's treatment of evil is thus consistent with Augustine of Hippo's explanation of it as a deprivation or corruption of good, as we have seen. Good and evil are not on the same plane. There can be no evil without a prior good to be corrupted. How does Tolkien portray that corruption in *The Hobbit*?

We see the profundity of evil in Morgoth, Ungoliant, Sauron, and Shelob. Perhaps we see in the Goblins something of the pettiness and cruelty to which evil can reduce those who yield to it. And we must picture their ancestors as those Elves who did yield to evil. Those who remained faithful to Iluvatar would have died from their treatment by Morgoth rather than becoming useful to him. A captured Elf who was not rescued would then either have ended as a martyr or a traitor. And this may explain the ferocity of the Elves' hatred of the Orcs as we will see it in the Trilogy. It may also be relevant to the question that has troubled many of why the Orcs seem to be treated as irredeemable. We will come back to it when we get to the Trilogy. But those are deeper waters than we are asked to swim in here.

Here, the Goblins are slavemasters who force their slaves to work until they die for lack of air and light. That is a practice wholly sufficient to mark them as the Bad Guys, but it is only the beginning. The slaves are toiling because the Goblins don't like to work with their hands. The Goblins have eschewed the sub-creation proper to creatures—the very opposite error to Feanor's and Turgon's, who loved the work of their own hands too much. And they are forcing their slaves to create things that are sometimes clever but never beautiful and which include what today we would call weapons of mass destruction: "ingenious devices for killing large numbers of people at once."[32] If these are marks of evil, then good people love light, respect the value of others' lives and their rights, and practice proper sub-creation—as we see Hobbits doing in their well-ordered farmland and Elves in

---

[32] *The Hobbit*, op. cit., 62.

their perfect house for food, sleep, work, story-telling, thinking by the fire, or all of them together. When in the Trilogy some of the Hobbits learn to appreciate the high and fair forms provided by the Elves and add them to the homeyness of the Shire, we will have an ideal of goodness to which even moral Men can aspire.

Bilbo now meets another embodiment of evil in Gollum, and their interactions provide the impetus for the rest of this story and beyond. The narration of the Riddle Game is really well written. Here's how I know. Every time I read it, I remember vividly the first time so long ago. Every single riddle stumped me. I didn't get even one of them, despite stopping and trying really hard after each one before I let myself read the solution. I didn't get a single one right, but every single one seemed kick-yourself obvious the second I gave up and let Gollum or Bilbo solve it for me. And I think that is just the effect Tolkien must have aimed for. Each riddle is a masterpiece of its own genre, and they work together to heighten the suspense.

Had I been in that cave, I would have ended up in Gollum's belly and he would still be using the Ring to snare wayward Goblins. So there was more to Bilbo than met the eye indeed, and the Ring was not the whole reason why.

# DAY 17

# The Hobbit

## *"Out of the Frying Pan" and "Queer Lodgings"*

"Escaping goblins to be caught by wolves" becomes a proverb, but one wonders why, since the wolves are also escaped from, and the escape from the wolves is one of the most exciting scenes in the book. How well written it is can be seen by comparing it with someone else's attempt to tell the same story. In Peter Jackson's version, the Dwarves just happen to fall out of their pine trees that are leaning over the Cliffs of Peril from *Monty Python and the Holy Graal* (ahem) right when Eagles just happen to be flying past right under them. And Jackson's Eagles must have feathers made out of velcro, for instead of bouncing off of them, the Dwarves somehow stick and get rescued in spite of the sheer impossibility of it's happening that way.

This is not an isolated problem. One recalls the Dwarves falling off a five-hundred-foot cliff in Jackson's version of the goblin cave and bounding up from the rocks below as if nothing had happened. Even Dwarves are not that tough, and nobody, not even Bilbo, is that lucky. Nor can Radagast's sled overcome the friction to run over dry leaves without any snow, even if it is pulled by Rabbits of Rhosgobel. As for drowning Smaug in a river of molten gold … Oh, never mind.

Here's the point: Tolkien added the laws of magic to the primary world in order to sub-create Middle-earth, but he did not subtract the laws of physics. I say this not to criticize Jackson so much as to highlight the excellence of the work Tolkien did to make our "willing suspension of disbelief" possible. His Eagles fly down and pluck the Dwarves and Bilbo from the trees like Eagles that have some sense. And it's a good thing, too. I wouldn't want either Tolkien or Jackson to have to describe the interior of a wolf's belly.

Once we do escape, we basically have to get the adventure restarted if we are to finish it. The answer to that need is Beorn's house. Beorn is the Bombadil of *The Hobbit*. The analogy is not perfect—Tom does not show up to add his power to any of the battles in *The Lord of the Rings* (though he does rescue the Hobbits from the Barrow Wight). But it is the same kind of interlude in a hauntingly magical place. And Beorn belongs in his realm the way Tom does in the Withywindle Valley. Gandalf uses the same strategy to get Bombadil to accept the company that he had used with the Dwarves arriving at Bag End for that fateful tea that got the whole Adventure started. It is absurd the number of readings I had done before I noticed that parallel. Perhaps that is one more bit of evidence of how fitting it seems for its own moment in the story, how skillful a writer Tolkien actually was.

One stumble: Despite all the praise of Tolkien as a writer of believable fantasy I've just expressed above, he was not perfect. I cannot *quite* suspend my disbelief in some of the feats performed by Beorn's animals. I do not doubt his ability as a trainer nor their willingness to serve, but not all their operations are anatomically possible for those species, however intelligent, well-trained, and well-intentioned.

Unless some of them are shape-shifters too? Hmmm …

## DAY 18

# The Hobbit

### *"Flies and Spiders"*

Has anybody warned us not to leave the path?

The feasting of the Elves, all the light, the food, the merry voices, the laughter, the music, seen and heard from a distance in the intolerable darkness of the Forest, but never reachable, vanishing the moment you think you have reached it: It is a classic image of what C. S. Lewis called *sehnsucht* or longing or Joy. Thorin's company has a terrible practical need for food and water at that point, so their attempts to grasp what they have glimpsed may be purely pragmatic. But the well-fed reader sees more, an evocation of the glimmers of glory that keep us always searching but never finding—not if we assume that what we are looking for is fully available in this world.

Tolkien does not talk about joy or longing in the same terms as Lewis (though his own concept of eucatastrophe is not unrelated). But his books evoke it as reliably as any that have ever been written. Lewis describes being hit out of the blue by the memory of a toy garden his brother Warnie had made out of twigs and moss on the lid of a biscuit tin and brought into the nursery, and which had been the young Lewis's first experience of the beauty of nature. The memory of that moment aroused a longing for something which neither the toy garden nor any real one could actually supply. It was gone as soon as it was aroused: "an unsatisfied desire which is itself more desirable than any satisfaction."[33] It was for Lewis a signpost ultimately facilitating the realization that there are spiritual realities that cannot be reduced to the atoms in motion that constitute the material world.

If we start with *The Hobbit*, we do not yet understand why the Elves are in themselves an embodiment of Lewis's theme. It is made more clear as we learn their backstory from the Trilogy and *The Silmarillion*: They are a part of this world that by their nature and their history points beyond it to the West, to Elvenhome and that which is beyond Elvenhome, the land of the Valar. We don't know this from *The Hobbit*, but already we begin to feel it (if we can forget "Tra lala lally"). These glimpses of elusive Elven beauty in Mirkwood give that feeling to many readers who do not yet understand the rationale behind it.

The spiders are, we now know, descendants of Ungoliant, the greatest evil, Morgoth and maybe Sauron only excepted, ever to befall Middle-earth. We see this in their stubborn attempts to recapture the Dwarves and capture Bilbo long after it should have been obvious that they were going to lose far more than they could gain by that effort, even if they succeeded. Real, proactive evil, not even unenlightened self-interest, is the only explanation for such behavior, and only a perverted pride can lie behind it, as has been true since the paradigmatic case of Satan. The Spiders are thus an even less humanized picture of evil than the Goblins, who were certainly bad enough. And immediately as a foil to it we get the Wood-Elves, good (but not perfect) people who show their basic goodness by being fairly "well be-

---

[33] C. S. Lewis, *Surprised by Joy: The Shape of my Early Life* (NY: Harcourt, Brace, & World, 1955): 17–18.

haved" even to their worst enemies.[34] Those who read this as children are getting a very basic lesson in the difference between civilization and barbarism—a lesson that adults will do well not to miss themselves.

---

[34] *The Hobbit*, op. cit., 168.

# DAY 19

# The Hobbit

### *"Barrels out of Bond"*

OK, it's time for the next rant about Peter Jackson's Hobbit movies that I've been putting off since the last one.

I didn't mind expanding the narrative via the back-story. That was a potentially interesting approach that could have been done well. But the face-palms started building up early. Rabbits of Rhosgobel who can pull a sledge over dry leaves with no snow? Is there not such a thing as friction in Middle-earth? Dwarves who fall off a 500-foot cliff and walk away as if nothing had happened? (As I noted above, Tolkien added the laws of Magic to his secondary world, but he did not subtract the laws of Physics.) Dwarves who randomly fall out of trees and just happen to land on the backs of Eagles who just happen to be flying under them at just the right moment? We add Legolas and Tauriel (whoever she is), and consequently these two Elvish ninjas must each slay more Orcs in each film than Sauron and Saruman between them ever bred? Face-palm, face-palm, face-palm. But up to now I was still hanging in there and looking for bits I could enjoy. And there were some. The music of the Dwarves' song in Bag End was just about perfect—the right mood in itself, and just the kind of song those Dwarves would sing.

Then we come to the current chapter. It was no worse than anything else, and I had certainly been led to expect it, But for whatever reason, the running archery battle between the Dwarves and the Orcs from the tubs in the Running River was the last straw—a straw that should have been packed into one of the tubs, if you will pardon the pun (or should I say, "if you take my meaning"). "Alright, that's it. I'm done," quoth I. "I can't take this anymore."

Just give me the story the way Tolkien wrote it, thag you very buch.

The way Tolkien wrote it, it is an important chapter in which the growth of Bilbo's character continues. Managing the escape from Gollum and the Goblins in the cave had already forced our hero to find capacities only Gandalf could have foreseen in the fat, respectable Hobbit of "The Unexpected Party." Then having a magic ring and an ancient sword had made a great difference in the battle with the Spiders. "I shall give you a name," he said to the little sword, "and I shall call you *Sting*."[35] Naming the sword is a way of identifying with the great heroes of the past, though Bilbo would hardly have put it to himself that way, as he is retaining the good part of his earlier innocence while jettisoning its comfortable naivety. Now, circumstances force him to take another step up, as it becomes clear that if anyone is going to rescue the Dwarves from prison and salvage their quest, "it would have to be done by Mr. Baggins, alone and unaided."[36]

We have to take the fat, self-satisfied Hobbit of chapter one and get him to the point where he can credibly take the crucial role he plays in the lead-up to the Battle of the Five Armies. It cannot be done all at once. This episode is an important step. We were told at the outset that we would see whether Bilbo gained

---

[35] Ibid., 155.
[36] Ibid., 173.

anything from his Adventure in the end to compensate for the loss of his reputation. The answer to that question is already starting to be revealed.

# DAY 20

# The Hobbit

## "A Warm Welcome" and "On the Doorstep"

These chapters begin with another example of Bilbo's famous "luck" (if luck you call it). Conditions had worsened in the Wild even since Gandalf's last trip, and the road the Dwarves had tried to take through Mirkwood now came to a very ambiguous end. The escape via barrels into the river had seemed like a desperate expedient, an uncomfortable escape, and an annoying detour, In fact, it had been the only way Lake Town could safely have been reached. "So you see, Bilbo had come in the end by the only road that was any good."[37] (189).

When Tolkien wrote that passage, he could have had no idea that his book would become immensely successful, leading to a popular demand for "more Hobbit" that would eventually lead to the wholly unplanned and unanticipated *Lord of the Rings*—to Tolkien's mind, just one more interruption to the more important work he needed to be doing on *The Silmarillion*. It is remarkable therefore how well this little passing statement feels like a planned foreshadowing of realities that could only be fully revealed when the Trilogy and its prequel were both available. Frodo also will come by the only road that is any good (as we will see when we

---

[37] Ibid., 189.

get there). It beautifully completes a pattern Tolkien could not have realized at the time that he was setting up.

But of course, Tolkien did understand that by setting his children's story in the Arda he had already created for *The Silmarillion*, he was setting it in a world in which forces for both good and evil were at work behind the scenes, and in which the forces for good were stronger in the long run. So when it turns out that Bilbo was meant to find the Ring, and not by its maker, this will be an encouraging thought—far more encouraging than Frodo is capable of perceiving when Gandalf says it. Bilbo's "luck," then, is not mere luck but is rooted in the nature of the world as Tolkien has subcreated it. You have the luck that goes along with the eucatastrophe of the Fairy Tale (see the essay "On Fairie Stories), but it is grounded in something more dependable than mere fortune. We will come back to this motif in another page or two.

Meanwhile, the Dwarves shock the Master of Lake Town by actually going to the Mountain (for there is no knowing what they will dare to do for revenge and the recovery of their property), they search in vain for the secret Door until Bilbo, Fili, and Kili find it, and then they sit of the doorstep interminably, being unable to get it open by any means they can think to try. Adventures have those periods of tedious waiting that fortunately take less time to tell about than to endure. Were it not for Bilbo (who also forgets them until the last minute) they would never have remembered the runes on the map. But he does remember, just in time for the last light of Durin's Day (more of his famous luck, if luck you call it), and the door is opened. What it leads to will be more than anyone has bargained for, but that is another chapter for another day.

# DAY 21

# The Hobbit

## *"Inside Information" and "Not at Home"*

"It does not do to leave a live dragon out of your calculations, if you live near him."[38] How the Inklings must have hooted at that little masterpiece of British understatement when Tolkien first read it to them. But it was no laughing matter for Bilbo and the Dwarves. Nor was it for the unfortunate citizens of Esgaroth, for if dragons can fly, then Lake Town certainly counts as "near." It was not just the Dwarves then who seem strangely unprepared for the evil that is awakened by the Quest. But what other outcome was there to expect? What was Gandalf thinking?

We know what the Lake people were thinking, except for Bard: The dragon is asleep and probably legendary and so we can go about our comfortable lives leaving him out of account because that is the easiest thing to do. What Gandalf was thinking is more complicated. There is evil in the world, dragons are among the ultimate embodiments of it, and it needs to be opposed. And this is not the only occasion where opposing evil made things worse before they got better. One thinks of the Children of Israel, who were rewarded for Moses demanding that Pharaoh let them go by getting to make bricks without straw as Pharaoh doubled down on their oppression. Yet this was a necessary step toward

---

[38] Ibid., 215.

their liberation. (Gandalf would not have known that story, but the readers should.) The loss of life and property and the deprivations suffered by the Lake Town folk were real and severe. Yes, evil needs to be opposed, but one normally should use some common sense in doing so. Is that happening here?

Is the suffering of Lake Town, in other words, just a risk we have to take? Not quite. One of the criteria of just war theory is that one's opposition to evil has to have some realistic chance of success so that it will save more lives than it costs. Does stirring Smaug up have any chance to meet that criterion? It might not seem so at first. But we learn eventually that Gandalf has been thinking ahead. If the dragon is not dealt with, imagine what might eventually take place: a greater devastation than the Battle of Five Armies if the Necromancer sends the Goblins and the Wargs against the free peoples with Smaug at their head. Then Elves, Dwarves, and Men would have been fighting a much greater force separately, not having been providentially brought together, and that might have meant the end of Lake Town and the Forest Kingdom and of the Iron Hills too. We cannot just sit and wait for that to happen!

This is all hinted at in the Appendix to *The Return of the King*, "Of Durin's Folk," in the Story of Gandalf's initial meeting with Thorin at Bree—"a chance meeting, as we say in Middle-earth."[39] As with luck, there is always more to chance in Middle-earth than may be apparent to outward sight. But in *The Hobbit* itself, we have to wonder—as we will keep doing in the next chapter.

---

[39] J. R. R. Tolkien, *The Return of the King* (NY: Ballantine, 1955): 411.

# The Hobbit

### *"Fire and Water" and "The Gathering of the Clouds"*

It did not bother me at first, but in subsequent readings I began to have the nagging doubt I started talking about in the chapter just above. What could possibly have made Gandalf think sending thirteen Dwarves and a Hobbit against a dragon could possibly lead to anything but disaster? What made anyone think that burglary was going to produce any effect other than it did—devastation for Lake Town and most likely for Thorin's company as well? Nobody could have predicted Bilbo's finding Smaug's unprotected spot, or that the Thrush would be there to tell Bard about it. How is Gandalf's plan anything more than just irresponsibly poking a hornet's nest in the insane hope that something good would somehow come of it? Kind of like sending two tom-fool Hobbits into Mordor with the Ring…

I don't think there is a complete answer to this problem in *The Hobbit* itself, though we hinted at a partial one in the last chapter. Only reading *The Lord of the Rings* in the light of *The Silmarillion* helps us fully to come to grips with it. For the same pattern plays out there, with Gandalf sending those two tom-fool Hobbits into Mordor with the Ring. But in those works taken together, we learn that, as a servant of the Secret Fire, Gandalf has insight into the will of Iluvatar that enables him to take risks that would *otherwise* have been insane. He may not foresee every detail of exactly how it is going to work, but he knows that Bilbo was meant to find the Ring and that this is an encouraging thought, and his heart tells him the Gollum has yet a role to play, for good or ill, and that Bilbo's (and Frodo's) mercy will rule the fate of many. Because as the Maia Olorin he was present at the Great Music and knows the End toward which all the deeds of Middle-earth arc, because he knows and trusts Iluvatar, he is able to set in motion processes that he himself does not fully understand and whose outcomes he cannot personally guarantee. In the biblical phrase whose inversion we saw to be a key to Numenorean unfaithfulness, Gandalf walks by faith and not by sight. It is not a blind faith: It is based on an understanding of who Iluvatar is and his memory of the Great Music. But it is faith, and not sight, for all that.

In *The Hobbit* we do not see the clues and the reasoning about them that underlie and justify Gandalf's confidence the way we do in the Trilogy. But having seen it in the Trilogy, we can believe that something adequate was there. Like Gandalf, we too as readers must walk by faith and not by sight.

# The Hobbit

## *"A Thief in the Night," and "The Clouds Burst,"*

Just a little humility on either side and there would have been no need for the confrontation of the Mountain versus the Lake and the Forest. Yet without their conflict, there would not have been three armies to face the Orcs and the Wargs, and the return to the Mountain would have been in vain. It is not just Bilbo who comes by what looks like the worst road possible that turns out to be the only road that is any good! A Hobbit, a Wizard, and three armies of Men, Elves, and Dwarves all manage to do just that, with nobody (apparently) planning it. Oft is it seen that good and evil, while clearly distinguishable, are mixed together in very messy ways. That is why, when good triumphs, there is always an element of eucatastrophe, that is, of surprising grace.

But eucatastrophe is not a Disneyfied "happily ever after." It must be surprising yet inevitable, unexpected yet uncontrived, extremely costly yet supremely worth the cost. Nobody at the Field of Cormallen will be able to deny the extremity of the cost of that victory, nor will anyone there be prone to doubt the supremity of its worth. As we saw above, realism about what the Necromancer might have done with Smaug had Gandalf not engineered his interference with those plans will help us recognize the same pattern being played out here, with the criterion of just war theory being met explicitly.

Despite the inevitable messiness, some things are clear. "There is more of good in you than you know, child of the kindly West.... If more of us valued good food and cheer and song above hoarded gold, it would be a merrier world,"[40] Thorin will say as he lies dying in the next chapter. So it would be. But a certain supply of troll gold allowed Bilbo to maintain his life, practice his legendary kindness to his nieces and nephews until he was eleven-one, and leave Frodo financially self-sufficient as the Master of Bag End despite the financial losses the old Hobbit had suffered at the auction on his return. There is a fine line between hoarding and stewardship. On that line there is a door, and the key that opens it to the right side is generosity. So Thorin was right on all counts. Oh. Would that be grace, again?

It would be.

---

[40] *The Hobbit*, op. cit., 288.

# DAY 25

# The Hobbit

## *"The Return Journey" and "The Last Stage"*

Let us take a moment to enjoy with Bilbo the more than half century of life he lived after his return until the opening of the Ring Trilogy before we charge ahead into it. The friendship of Elves, the honor of Dwarves and Wizards, the blowing of smoke-rings, and the writing of poetry: That is a loss of "reputation" to which we can all aspire!

The last couple of poems, the elves' "Sing All Ye Joyful" and Bilbo's "Roads Go Ever. Ever On,"[41] are the best we have heard since the Dwarves'"Far Over the Misty Mountains Cold."[42] They quite take the bad taste of "Tra-la-la-lally" out of our mouths, and they also anticipate the exquisite compositions we will be treated to in the Trilogy. When the last one moves Gandalf to note that Bilbo is not the Hobbit he was, we have to remember the very un-Tookish Avoider of Adventures of the opening scenes with a smile. Bilbo has been late for quite a few dinners and has as a result become what literary critics call a "dynamic character," one who grows and develops in ways spurred by and consistent with the plot. Indeed, he is one of the most dynamic characters in literature by that description. This is somewhat

---

[41] Ibid., 297–8, 300.
[42] Ibid., 13–15.

ironic, as Tolkien is often accused by the perversely dense of filling his world with "flat characters." One wonders what sort of blinders such readers can be wearing.

The Hobbit closes with a hint of more serious adventures to come in the Trilogy and the serious themes that will accompany them. Balin and Gandalf visit Bilbo in the Shire, and they sit reminiscing about their adventures. Bilbo marvels that the prophecies of the old songs really came true. Why shouldn't they? Gandalf asks. Why does Bilbo's own role in bringing these things about make the prophecies less than prophecies and their fulfillment less than fulfillment? They were not managed by mere luck just for Bilbo's personal benefit! Even though the phrase does not appear, the context implies it: Luck and chance are rarely mentioned without someone to add, "If luck/chance you call it." It is a light and jocular moment, as Bilbo laughs and hands Gandalf the tobacco jar.[43] But it hints of larger vistas and more cosmic purposes lurking in the background. These hints are going to be fulfilled.

OK, tomorrow, *The Fellowship of the Ring*.

---

[43] Ibid., 303.

## DAY 26

# The Fellowship of the Ring
### *"An Unexpected Party"*

Tolkien as usual is really good at opening chapters. My first time through the Trilogy, I had not read *The Hobbit*. I plunged right in with only the summary in the Prologue as background. It was not a problem. Everything I learned about Hobbits in the first pages was brand new to me, yet it felt like I had known it all forever. Both stories begin with a party: one unexpected and one planned in great detail with much anticipation. And it is appropriate: Both books will be more fun than a Birthday Party. I might need to post a notice at the head of my own chapter about that chapter, a *caveat lector*, as it were: NO ADMITTANCE EXCEPT ON PARTY BUSINESS!

I've averaged reading it annually since 1968, yet still there are passages in "An Unexpected Party" that render me helpless. I know they are coming, and they still get me every time. A couple of examples:

> But old Rory Brandybuck wasn't so sure. Neither age nor an enormous dinner had clouded his wits, and he said to his daughter-in-law Esmeralda, 'There's something fishy in this, my dear. I believe that mad Baggins is off again. Silly old fool. But why worry? He hasn't taken the vittles with him.'[44]

---

[44] *FOTR*, op. cit., 53.

Now, why is that so funny? I see that it is funny, but why should it be practically incapacitating? I hooted my head off at it again, as loudly as I did the first time. The Gaffer hoping that no harm will come of Mt. Bilbo having taught Sam his letters is on the same level.[45] How the Inklings, perhaps the most lettered club in the history of letters and clubs, must have hooted at that!

From the ridiculous to the sublime: It's a simple sentence that lays me low every year. When Bilbo finally leaves, "He jumped over a low place in the hedge at the bottom and took to the meadows, passing into the night like a rustle of wind in the grass."[46] Something about that last simile leaves me weeping like a baby every time. Shakespeare gets the same effect with Prospero's speech:

> Our revels now are ended. These our players
> Were, as I foretold you, all spirits
> And are vanished into air, into thin air.
> And like the baseless fabric of this vision,
> The cloud-capped towers, the gorgeous palaces,
> The solemn temples, yea, the great globe itself
> And all that in inherit shall dissolve
> And like this insubstantial pageant faded
> Leave not a wrack behind. We are such stuff
> As dreams are made on, and our little life
> Is rounded with a sleep.[47]

Shakespeare expends all the massive powers of his rhetoric to capture the intolerably poignant beauty-in-brevity of mortal life, and it is brilliant; but Tolkien gets the same punch from a simple phrase that lies in wait for its unsuspecting victim with no fanfare whatsoever. Neither age nor fifty-seven years of read-

---

[45] Ibid., 44.
[46] Ibid., 58.
[47] William Shakespeare, "The Tempest," IV.1.148–58.

ing have dulled my wits to Tolkien's magic. I will not say, "Do not weep," for not all tears are an evil.

# DAY 27

# The Fellowship of the Ring
## *"The Shadow of the Past"*

"The Shadow of the Past" shows off Tolkien's great talent for atmospherics. The hushed foreboding in the darkened room perfectly sets off the somber back-story of the Ring and keeps it from being a mere infodump. Then Sam brings us back to the present by being whisked in through the window to join the quest, and we know it is real and will have real consequences for the life these hobbits have known.

Meanwhile, this chapter is one of the most important in the Trilogy from a thematic point of view. Tolkien does not just reveal the facts we need to know about the back story; he has Gandalf comment on their meaning in ways that lay out some of the most significant motifs we are to encounter and set us up to understand them as one of the Wise.

One of them is a serious and unromantic view of evil as represented by Sauron and focused in the Ring. It is powerful; it is corrupting; mortal wills cannot resist it unaided; it must be opposed anyway; and there is no final victory over it in this life. "Always, after a defeat and a respite, the Shadow takes another shape and grows again."[48] There is an eschatological end for

---

[48] Ibid., 76.

Middle-earth in which the Final Chord of the Great Music will bring resolution and peace and the brazen notes of Morgoth will be overcome.[49] But Frodo knows nothing of that, and Gandalf only hints at it. Frodo must find the courage to do his part in the battle without any assurance of final victory. Even the destruction of the Ring will not be such a victory, not yet. It will only provide the next Respite.

This, by the way, is the key to the alleged conflict between paganism and Christianity in Tolkien which has puzzled so many.[50] There is no ultimate conflict because the pagan, pessimistic view *is* the Christian view of *this* age of the world. What paganism lacks is the Christian hope that it will not always be thus. But for now, the Christian like Tolkien who understands the Christian's eschatological hope is able thereby to avoid stupidly calling World War I "the war to end all wars" and thus avoid being disillusioned when World War II is its inevitable sequel. Thus we are able much better to decide "what to do with the time that is given us."[51]

Meanwhile, we fight for the right, with force when necessary, but we also get the first hints that something else might be the ultimate key to victory. "Pity? It was Pity that stayed [Bilbo's] hand. Pity and Mercy, not to strike without need."[52] Bilbo's sparing Gollum back in the Goblin cave will indeed become the most important destiny-shaping act of the whole saga, in ways that nobody could have predicted. But we are able to continue the struggle in hope because "Bilbo was meant to find the Ring, and not by its maker." In that room, only Gandalf understands

---

[49] For a full development of this theme, see Donald T. Williams, "A Far Green Country: The Eschatology of Tolkien's Middle-earth," *Theology and Tolkien: Constructive Theology*, ed. Douglas Estes (NY: Lexington Books/Fortress Academic, 2024): 301–15.

[50] Compare our treatment of this issue in the chapter on "The Valaquenta."

[51] FOTR, op. cit., 76.

[52] Ibid., 85.

why this is an "encouraging thought."[53] But the reader who has come by way of *The Silmarillion* will realize that, while we must not expect a final victory today, Middle-earth has not been abandoned. There is another Power at work who does know everything about Hobbits, and everything else as well. That Power will give Frodo the courage to decide what to do, and it will give us the courage, in spite of all the darkness of this shadowy chapter, to turn the page.

---

[53] Ibid., 81.

# DAY 28

# The Fellowship of the Ring
## *"Three is Company"*

I have always wondered: given the seriousness of what has just been revealed, why isn't there more urgency to get Frodo and the Ring quietly out of the Shire? Sure, they have to set their escape up not to look suspicious, and that will take some time. But hanging around until September seems like just inviting disaster. I guess hindsight is 20/20. Note to self: Next time you need to bug out ahead of nine Wraiths of Evil, Donald, do not waste the weeks when they have not yet appeared saying goodbye to your favorite hiking trails in Toccoa!

Once we get the Adventure started, we get three of the best poems in the Trilogy. (For those who understand, like Tolkien and the Hobbits, Adventures and Poetry go together. They have done since Homer.) The best commentary on "The road goes ever on and on" is Bilbo's, as Frodo remembers it. I can't resist quoting it in full:

> He used to say that there was only one Road, that is was like a great river; its springs were at every doorstep, and every path was its tributary. "It's a dangerous thing, Frodo, going out of your door," he used to say. "You step into the Road, and if you don't keep your feet, no knowing where you might be swept off

to. Do you realize that this is the very path that goes through Mirkwood, and that if you let it, it might take you to the Lonely Mountain, or even further and to worse places?"[54]

One of the great gifts Tolkien gives us is the ability to see the world like that.

"Upon the hearth the fire is red" depicts the perfect relationship to the great Road, which normal people not called upon to be heroes can enjoy: It is always there for us with its access to the world and to little Adventures, but rooted in hearth and home.[55] Then the hymn to Elbereth hints of heights that await us on the current heroic journey.[56] It also has a more immediate function to perform in the development of an important character.

To wit: After the encounter with Gildor Inglorion's folk, Frodo asks Sam how he likes Elves now that he has met them. Sam gives the first hint of the wisdom of which he will become capable with a truly profound reply: "They seem a bit above my likes and dislikes, so to speak."[57] (It's actually early in the next chapter, but it is Sam's response to what happens in this one, so I discuss it here).

What is Sam saying? There are values that transcend personal feelings. What the Elves are in themselves, in other words, is more important than how he feels about them. They were not put into Middle-earth to be the subject of his approval or disapproval. Perhaps he needs to be silent before something so high and fair and simply absorb it rather than chattering about it. Maybe constant commentary is not the highest form of homage. Then again, maybe I actually need to listen to Sam's wisdom and apply it to this statement!

---

[54] Ibid., 102.
[55] Ibid., 106–7.
[56] Ibid., 108.
[57] Ibid., 117.

This, it seems to me, is the only proper response to many things in life. It is not one we hear a lot from modern and post-modern people. Let me hear it more from myself. (But never fear: It will not stop me from finishing this book, though maybe it will keep me from being too prolix in the process.)

DAY 29

# The Fellowship of the Ring
### *"A Short Cut to Mushrooms"*
### *and "A Conspiracy Unmasked"*

Tolkien's good guys are really good. This is not just a tautology. I mean that they are well drawn and that they are drawn in such a way as to expose the lie (which no doubt goes back to Morgoth) that goodness is boring. From Elrond's creation of the perfect house to the nobility of Aragorn and Faramir to the lofty beauty of Galadriel to the sacrificial love of Frodo and Sam, Tolkien shows us goodness in an eye-opening variety of styles, forms, personalities, and manifestations. He also lets us find it in unexpected places. Here the down-home, rustic solidity of Farmer Maggot is the vehicle of that theme.

You would have thought that the effect of the Black Rider on his dogs would have been enough to tell Maggot that he wants nothing to with such specters and will do absolutely nothing to attract their further attention or risk getting on their bad side. What it in fact tells him to do is to take Frodo into his home, sit him at his table, take him to the ferry in his wagon—and, oh, yes, leave the young rascal of memory with a basket of mushrooms. That last touch is the *piece de resistance* of a masterpiece of a portrait. Maggot knows nothing about what is at stake, but he knows what the right thing to do is, and he'll be damned if any sinister figure, no matter how threatening, is going to intimidate him out of doing it. All this in a minor character we are not going to see again. We need to meet such people in our journeys, and we need to be such people in the journeys of others.

"A Conspiracy Unmasked" is one of my favorite chapters. I think C. S. Lewis's treatment of friendship in *The Four Loves* is interesting and insightful but incomplete, and Tolkien here adds what was missing. Lovers stand face to face looking at each other, Lewis explains. Friends stand side by side looking together at something else.[58] Lewis's exposition of common interest as the essence of friendship is important and foundational, but in true friendship it leads to a level of loyalty and fidelity that transcends it. I know someone has the potential to be a great friend when my comment to myself is, "This person loves the right things for the right reasons." I know that the potential is going to be fully realized when he shows the steadfast character that should flow from those loves. And each of us reliably showing it when the other is in need is essential too.

Lewis does not deny this, but Tolkien brings it out forcefully in one of the classic portrayals of all time. The bath song is the perfect comic relief for the seriousness that comes to expression in Merry's response to Frodo's exclamation, "It does not seem that I can trust anyone."[59]

"It all depends on what you mean," put in Merry. "You can trust us to stick to you through thick and thin—to the bitter end. And you can trust us to keep any secret of yours—closer than you keep it yourself. But you cannot trust us to let you face trouble alone and go off without a word. We are your friends, Frodo."

Yes.

---

[58] C. S. Lewis, *The Four Loves* (NY: Harcourt, Brace, & World, 1960): 91.
[59] FOTR, op, cit., 138.

# DAY 30

# The Fellowship of the Ring
## *"The Old Forest" and "In the House of Tom Bombadil"*

The Old Forest when we first encounter it is dark, oppressive, and hostile, vaguely evil, but nothing you can put your finger on. When we get to Fangorn, we realize that it sounds an awful lot like a population of rogue Huorns isolated and cut off from any Ents. It sends the Hobbits down to the Withywindle valley— clean out of the way—but only so do they meet Bombadil and end up crossing the Barrow Downs and acquiring some swords that turn out to be pretty significant later on. The old habit of blundering into the only way that was really any good turns out to be hard to break, even across generations!

I tried hard to remember my initial reaction to Bombadil, and while many moments of my first reading so many years ago are still as fresh as May morning, that one has escaped me. He is so strange and such an outlier, different from anything else in the work, that I wonder at that lapse of memory. Elves, Dwarves, Goblins, wraiths, trolls, dragons—we have met them all before, and while Tolkien's may have original takes on these species, he did not start from scratch in creating them. If Bombadil has antecedents in earlier fantasy, they were not obvious to me. But Middle-earth contains so many strange and wonderful creatures who all seem to be perfectly at home in their own bits of it, that maybe I was just glad to be rescued from Old Man Willow and put off wondering about Tom until later.

OK, it's later. So who (or what) the heck *is* Tom Bombadil? Both he and Treebeard are called the oldest. Treebeard is the oldest living creature still alive in Middle-earth, but Bombadil was present even before there were such creatures—he "knew the dark under the stars when it was fearless—before the Dark Lord came from the Outside."[60] This sounds like a reference to Morgoth rather than Sauron, and if so, it puts Tom in Middle-earth before the awakening of sentient creatures. So I suppose he and Treebeard can both be "eldest" if they are so in different categories. That would seem to make Tom one of the Valar or the Maiar. The effortless ease with which he overcomes the Barrow Wight suggests a Vala rather than a Maia. (Compare the Maia Gandalf's struggle to defeat the Balrog, a creature on the same level.) But Tom's personality fits none of the Valar (or Maiar, for that matter) that we are introduced to in the Valaquenta.

The closest thing we get to a hint is Tolkien's statement to Stanley Unwin that Tom is "the spirit of the (vanishing) Oxford and Berkshire countryside."[61] This is suggestive, but it does not help us fit Tom into the cast of beings we know about in Arda. Based on that suggestion, the closest we can get to understanding Tom is by taking the lovely walk on the Thames River Path in Oxford, from Port Meadow out past Godstowe Abbey to the Trout Inn. You will definitely feel that Tom belongs there, but when you get back to Oxford you will still find him as puzzling as he is delightful. The last word must then be Tolkien's statement

---

[60] Ibid., 168.
[61] Tolkien, *Letters*, op. cit., 26.

to Naomi Mitchison that "even in a mythical Age there must be some enigmas," and "Tom Bombadil is one (intentionally)."[62]

An enigma? I think we must finally say that in this as in most things concerning Middle-earth, Tolkien's intentions were fulfilled.

---

[62] Ibid., 174.

# DAY 31

# The Fellowship of the Ring
## *"Fog on the Barrow Downs" and "The Sign of the Prancing Pony"*

"Fog on the Barrow Downs" begins with Frodo's prescient dream vision of "a far green country spread out before him under a swift sunrise,"[63] a vision we will not see again until the very last page of the Trilogy. It heightens by contrast the cold, unseeing non-vision of the fogged-in Barrow Downs, as sinister a place as imagination has ever given us. I don't know what a barrow wight is, and I'm not sure I want to know any more than what Tom Shippey can tell us: "Barrow wights are familiar in Norse saga as ghosts, or more accurately, walking corpses, coming out of their grave mounds for vengeance on the living."[64] Tolkien of course has made them worse than that, if possible, combining the horror of the undead with a dragon's lust for gold and the mystery of an evil so dark and ancient that we know not what it is. We eventually discover its connections with the witch-king of Angmar, whose evil spell lingers ages after its destruction of the North Kingdom. It's a good thing it was on the borders of Bombadil's country, or the quest would have ended right there.

---

[63] FOTR, op. cit., 172.
[64] Tom Shippey, *J. R. R. Tolkien: Author of the Century* (Boston: Houghton Mifflin, 2000): 61.

Utterly incapable of capturing the eerie darkness of these spirits, I settle for the silliness of a Clerihew:

> A Barrow Wight
> Could give a person quite a fright.
> But if you can survive, his horde
> Might yield a pretty decent sword.[65]

"At the Sign of the Prancing Pony" is a real tour de force of
a chapter. Butterbur's inn has one of the most complicated and
compelling atmospheres of any place in literature. How does it
manage to be homey and mysterious, comfortable but with an
edge of danger, familiar and exotic, all at the same time? The combination is irresistibly intriguing. It is one of many places in Middle-earth, along with Bag End, Rivendell, and Loth Lorien, that
readers have a visceral hunger for, a desire that the place should
exist so they could visit it, a desire that hardly ever reaches the
same intensity in any other book.

An hour or two in the common room with a pint and a pipe
and a few good friends and someone singing "The Man in the
Moon Came Down too Soon" in the background would close a
hole in the psyche that you didn't know you had. Sharing news
with a transient Dwarf might not be "sure as Shiretalk," but it
would surely beat FOX or CNN. To gaze at the crowd from a
corner table with eyes shaded by Aragorn's hood would provide
a perspective on life that many volumes of philosophy and psychology could never give you. The Eagle and Child or the Lamb
and Flag[66] can whet this appetite, but they cannot fully satisfy
it. The fact that the Prancing Pony does not exist anywhere in a
world we can reach is one of those inconsolable wounds that we
are somehow grateful that Tolkien gave us. It is Lewis's *sehn-*

---

[65] Williams, *Stars through the Clouds*, op. cit., 286.
[66] Pubs in Oxford frequented by the Inklings.

*sucht* on steroids. *Sehnsucht* is not supposed to be predictable, but The Pony gets us every time.

# DAY 32

# The Fellowship of the Ring
## *"Strider"*

"Strider" is a well-written chapter that reveals Aragorn's identity and character, hugely important to the plot as they will be, in ways that also tell you more about the danger from the Riders and the growing up that the hobbits still need to do. It plays insightfully with universal literary themes like appearance and reality. "All that is gold does not glitter" is a warning not to trust too easily to appearances that coordinates with seeming foul and feeling fair and vice versa. The lesson seems to be that one should listen to one's instincts and not take all appearances at face value. Aragorn has to practice such discernment as well as the hobbits. He is concerned that they might be a trap set for him by the Enemy. The times call upon us to make such decisions, but not to become cynical and trust no one. At some point the risk of trust has to be taken on the best basis you can find, and no matter how good the basis, it will still be a risk.

"Strider" also contains one of the very few flaws in Tolkien's writing, which inspires one of only two changes to the story by Peter Jackson that actually make sense rather than simply introducing unnecessary lameness in the pursuit of superfluous drama. I am not slow to criticize Jackson, so I had better acknowledge his good judgment in this case.

I am not in Aragorn's league as a hiker and an outdoorsman, but I have done some pretty serious backpacking and covered significant segments of the Appalachian Trail on overnights extending upwards of four days. I have slept under the stars on mountain tops that only your feet can take you to. I have had to thaw the frozen water in my canteen before I could drink it of a morning. I have seen any number of Robert Frost's roads diverge in yellow woods, and generally taken the path less traveled by. And this I know: No hiker as skilled as Aragorn is going to be carrying one ounce of useless dead weight, and no Ranger pursued across Wilderland by all the servants of the Enemy is going to be carrying a sword he cannot use to defend himself. It actually makes more sense for Anduril to be in a shrine in Rivendell until it is reforged.

Tolkien went for the immediate effect of Aragorn's confirming his identity to Sam by conveniently pulling out the sword of the Rhyme (which was in the letter that also showed up just at the right moment to have the maximum effect). It works in the moment, but once you think about the realities that have to be faced before and after that moment, it makes no sense at all. Tolkien didn't think that scene through sufficiently, I'm afraid. We should be aware of this. We should also be aware that it is the very rarity of such lapses that make this one stand out and (if you will pardon the expression) cut so sharply.

Almost every reference to Peter Jackson in these reports will be a complaint, so I need to give him credit for the rare moment when he actually got something (other than scenery and architecture) right.

And what was the second change Jackson made that actually makes sense? Ah, I think I'll keep that secret until we get there.

# The Fellowship of the Ring
## *"A Knife in the Dark" and "Flight to the Ford"*

Frodo's unfortunate yielding to the highly suspicious urge to put on the Ring during the Black Riders' attack beneath Weathertop earns him a terrifying glimpse of the wraith-world and a Morgul-wound that threatens to ruin everything. Yet his yielding is mixed with a defiance that keeps it from being fatal, and it begins the long process of his struggle with the effects of the Ring that help to give him the empathy with Gollum that contributes to the mercy that rules the fate of many and is the ultimate key to victory. It is a mercy he can no longer remember that makes the difference at Sammath Naur, not his strength, which again is overcome. The complexities and the depths of the battle between good and evil in the individual soul that we see so profoundly in both Frodo and Gollum have their foundations laid here.

Arwen replaces Glorfindel in the Jackson movie because he needed to economize on characters and because of the desire to add some more masculine, butt-kicking capacity in a female role. But Tolkien already has Eowyn if we feel a need for that kind of thing, and given what happened to Arwen's mother (captured, tortured, and killed by orcs), it is hard to imagine Elrond ever allowing his daughter to participate in any such shenanigans. Her brothers Elladan and Elrohir's forwardness in such adventures makes perfect sense, though. As usual, Tolkien gets it right.

As we finish Book I, Asfaloth has just got Frodo across the Bruinen in the nick of time, and the Black Riders have been un-horsed, caught between Glorfindel and Elrond's surging river flood, as we will soon discover. "A knife in the Dark" and "Flight to the Ford" seem pretty grim only because we have not yet had to live through the Redhorn pass or Moria or the last desperate trek through Mordor. Sam's Troll song is the perfect (and needed) comic relief along the way. These chapters help to prepare us for what is coming. Right now, we just feel that we need the Last Homely House almost as much as Frodo does.

I try to imagine the reception the Nine will get when they make it back to Mordor. Never mind; let's not. They are ruled by the same terror they inspire in others, and their master cannot be happy with them. How many times have they let the Ring slip through their fingers? Hobbiton, Crickhollow, Weathertop, the Ford. Are they really that incompetent, or are we seeing the truth in Gandalf's belief that Bilbo was *meant* to find the Ring, and not by its maker? There is something else at work, indeed. The great advantage of starting with *The Silmarillion* is that we know what it is.

Tolkien has to walk a fine line in writing these episodes. We need narrow escapes both for the sake of suspense and to embody the motif of Iluvatar's Providence, but we have to keep them just plausible enough that we do not disturb the willing suspension of disbelief. You only see how fine the line is when you stop to think about it. While you are in each of those moments, you just believe. Walking that line without stepping over it is truly one of the more impressive marks of Tolkien's genius.

# DAY 34
# The Fellowship of the Ring
## *"Many Meetings"*

The last we knew, Frodo was losing consciousness amidst the cha-os of Elrond's river flood unhorsing the pursuing Nazgul. Then to our great relief he wakes up in bed in Rivendell to the voice of the long-missed Gandalf. After the horror of the Barrows, the tension of the chase across Wilderland, and the excitement of the escape at the Ford, this is a chapter in which practically noth-ing happens. But we do not need anything to happen. We are in Rivendell, and that is enough.

So let us just be in Rivendell for a while. But first, we must deal with the fact that the text of the third paragraph from the end of the third page of "Many Meetings" has become garbled somehow in the Ballantine paperback. Gandalf's answer should read as fol-lows: "That is just what the Rangers are: the last remnant in the North of the great people, the Men of the west. They have helped me before, and I shall need their help in the days to come; for we have reached Rivendell, but the Ring is not at rest."[67]

Nobody captures the sheer goodness that still adheres even in Arda Marred better than Tolkien in *The Lord of the Rings*: poig-nant and piercing, high and homely, serendipitous and simple,

---

[67] FOTR, op. cit.,., 267.

it breaks through on page after page to stop the heart and then start it up again, stronger than ever before. In no place is this goodness more evident than Rivendell, the Last Homely House West of the Mountains and East of the Sea. It was still as Bilbo had found it long ago, "a perfect house, whether you like food or sleep or story-telling or singing or just sitting and thinking best, or a pleasant mixture of them all."[68] There could be no better place for Frodo to wake up after escaping the Riders to be healed of his Morgul wound. There could be no better place to be even if you have no Morgul wound to be healed of.

In "Many Meetings," there are many good things to experience: healing, reunions with friends, rest, the clearing up of what had happened to Gandalf, food, music, and poetry. But that goodness finds its most concentrated moment in the reunion of Frodo and Bilbo: "They spoke no more of the small news of the Shire far away, nor of the dark shadows and perils that encompassed them, but of the fair things they had seen in the world together, of the Elves, of the stars, of trees, and the gentle fall of the bright year in the woods."[69]

Yes. This is why Sauron needs to be defeated and the Shire needs to be saved. Lots of writers can give us conflict, suspense, mystery, and stirring action. Tolkien can do that too, but nobody matches him in what he does here: showing us why winning those battles matters.

---

[68] Ibid., 272.
[69] Ibid., 286–7.

# DAY 35

# The Fellowship of the Ring
## *"The Council of Elrond"*

"The Council of Elrond" contains more information about the history of Middle-earth than anyone else besides Tolkien could have crammed into one chapter without eyes starting to glaze over. After more than fifty readings, mine still stay wide open (quite a feat for a mortal in Rivendell, apparently). One reason is the skill of the writing, the way everything comes out naturally from a variety of messengers, none of whom (except maybe Gandalf) has any idea what any of the others are going to say. Another reason that I particularly noticed this year is the role this chapter plays in the structure of the epic which is *The Lord of the Rings*.

I chose the word *epic* advisedly. We begin *in medias res* with Bilbo's Birthday Party, which serves to remind us that he still has the Ring and to arouse our curiosity about what this means and why handing it on to Frodo is such a challenge. The process of answering those questions starts in "The Shadow of the Past" and comes to a climax here. This is Odysseus at Alkinoos's banquet filling in the Phaiakians on the backstory of *The Odyssey*. (It is not a coincidence that there was a banquet the night before the Council, with Bilbo in the Hall of Fire playing the role of Demodokos. Does that make Arwen Nausikaa?) It is also reminiscent of Aeneas doing the same thing at Dido's banquet in *The Aeneid*.

Tolkien changes it up by splitting the infodump between seven characters (Bilbo, Frodo, Elrond, Gandalf, Gloin, Boromir, Legolas), each of whom has a different agenda, but all of whose contributions (*mirabile dictu!*) fit together into a coherent whole unplanned by any of them. Even Gandalf had not coordinated the contributions of Gloin, Borormir, and Legolas in advance. Both the similarities to Homer and Virgil and the differences work together to make what might have been a black hole of backstory hold our interest all the way through.

Not only does no one character orchestrate the revelations; no one present has orchestrated the meeting itself. Elrond says that the members of the Council have been called together, though he did not call them. They are all brought there by what seems to be chance, but it is not so; rather, it is "ordered" that they and no others shall take counsel for the peril that faces the world.[70] As with Bilbo being meant to find the Ring, the trilogy in itself constantly raises questions without answering them. Meant? By whom? Ordered? By whom? "The Ainulindale" in *The Silmarillion* makes plain the answer: It could be none else than Iluvatar. But within *The Lord of the Rings* itself, Tolkien is consistent with the strategy he laid out in the famous letter: It is a fundamentally Christian work, but the religious element is never explicit. It is "absorbed into the story."[71]

This chapter then gives us another example of how that absorption is done. It is done in a way that is appropriate to a world that is before the Old Testament, and it invites the reader to make the application for himself. Sometimes it is more effective to raise questions than to answer them.

Brilliant!

---

[70] Ibid., 291.
[71] Tolkien, *Letters*, op. cit., 172.

# DAY 36
# The Fellowship of the Ring
## *"The Ring Goes South"*

Tolkien has so many moments in which he captures the precise poignance of the human condition: the strange mix of joy and sorrow that comes from living with the Doom of Men in time amongst the beauties of Arda and the tragedies of Arda Marred. Bbilbo's farewell song in "The Ring Goes South" is one of those moments.

> I sit beside the fire and think
> Of all that I have seen:
> Of meadow flowers and butterflies
> In summers that have been,
> Of yellow leaves and gossamer
> In autumns that there were
> With morning mist and silver sun
> And wind upon my hair.
>
> I sit beside the fire and think
> Of how the world will be
> When winter comes without a spring
> That I shall ever see.
> For there are still so many things
> That I have never seen:
> In ever wood, in every spring,
> There is a different green.

I sit beside the fire and think
Of people long ago
And people who will see a world
That I shall never know.
But all the while I sit and think
Of times that were before,
I listen for returning feet
And voices at the door.[72]

The impossibility of holding on to anything as we pass through the world, which somehow makes us love it more, not less, climaxing with the most valuable thing of all, our relationships: It is the essence of mortal existence captured in simple purity. We see beauty from afar, but when we try to grasp it we step into the circle of light and the fires go out and we are thrust back into the pathless darkness of Mirkwood. We have real friends, and they are the best gift life has to offer, but at some point the Quest goes on and takes them with it and leaves us behind (or takes us and leaves them behind). In either case it leaves us wondering how in the world we got to that point in life so quickly. Shakespeare got it too: "This thou perceivest, which makes thy love more strong / To love that well which thou must leave e'er long."[73]

Gerard Manley Hopkins held to the hope that these goods we have to leave behind are kept for us far with fonder a care than we could have kept them, where? Yonder, yonder ... yonder.[74] And Aragorn lived by the hope that beyond the circles of the world is more than memory. Were they right? Read Bilbo's poem again and realize afresh how very much the answer to that question matters.

---

[72] FOTR, op. cit., 233–4.

[73] Shakespeare, Sonnet 73

[74] Gerard Manley Hopkins, "The Leaden Echo and the Golden Echo." *The Poems of Gerard Manley Hopkins*, ed. W. H. Gardner and N. H. MacKenzie (London: Oxford Univ. Pr., 1967): 93.

Meanwhile the Quest itself is no picnic. The Company is defeated by Caradhras, and things are not going to get easier any time soon.

# The Fellowship of the Ring
### *"A Journey in the Dark"*

"A Journey in the Dark" is not the most inspiring chapter in *The Lord of the Rings*. The darkness and the depths of Moria are oppressive to everyone except Gimli, and the ruin and desolation of it are depressing even to him. But that does not mean there are no important truths revealed there.

Every race of the free peoples has a heavy burden of loss to carry. The Elves have Rivendell, Lorien, and the Forest Kingdom, but not Nargothrond, Doriath, or Gondolin—whose greatness can never be recaptured, not even with rings on the fingers of Elrond and Galadriel. Minas Tirith looks out over the ruins of Osgiliath and across to the horror of what should be the lovely Minas Ithil; and King's Norbury is a waste. The Dwarves have their kingdom under the Mountain, but they will never again match what they had in Moria, in Khazad-Dum; there will be no more mithril for them to work with since they delved too deeply and greedily and awoke Durin's Bane. Legolas and Gimli develop a friendship for the ages, but Elves and Dwarves as races will never recover the relationship they had in a simpler world where "Speak 'friend' and enter" was a sufficient password.

Finally, as a last stake driven through the heart to nail down this lesson, Balin's attempt to reestablish a Dwarf kingdom in

Moria is found to have ended in a tomb in the Chamber of Mazarbul. Truly, Wordsworth could have been a bard for any of those peoples: "There hath passed away a glory from the earth."[75]

I hear the echo of Ulmo's voice echoing down the years into those dark, hollow spaces: "Love not too well the work of thine own hands." Do the work for its own sake and for the sake of those you love and whom you can serve with it—but do not expect it to last, do not cling to it for the sake of your own glory. If you do not heed the message of Ulmo, you will be left with the legacy of Ozymandias.

> "My name is Ozymandias, king of kings.
> Look on my works, ye mighty, and despair!"
> Nothing beside remains. 'Round the decay
> Of that colossal wreck, boundless and bare,
> The lone and level sands stretch far away.[76]

Is this the inevitable end of everything? No. We must remember the other part of Ulmo's message: Hope comes from the West. Gandalf and Aragorn will not forget this. Faramir is still remembering it. The rest of us are here to learn what it means. And so the Quest continues.

---

[75] William Wordsworth, "Ode" Intimations of Immortality from Recollections of early Childhood," *English Romantic Poetry and Prose*, ed. Russel Noyes ((NY: Oxford Univ, Pr., 1956): 327.

[76] Percy Bysshe Shelley, "Ozymandias," *English Romantic Poetry and Prose*, op. cit., 981.

DAY 38

# The Fellowship of the Ring
## *"The Bridge of Khazad-Dum"*

When I first read "The Bridge of Khazad-Dum" in the summer of 1968, the death of Gandalf was one of the two most devastating moments that literature had provided for my young life up to that time. Its only rival was the moment at the end of *1984* when Winston loves Big Brother.[77] That had come only a few months before. Orwell's scene was worse in some ways: more depressing, carrying with it the threat of an existential collapse at the realization of the epistemological vulnerability of the modern world.

What was the threatened collapse? Winston had known the truth. He had known that the lies of Big Brother were lies, and he had known that he knew it. But where was that knowledge? *What* was that knowledge? Just a few flickering neurons inside his skull. And if that is all truth is, it is helpless against the power of the Ministry of Truth and destined to extinction in any case.

This is not just a theoretical and fictional problem. I would realize that just a few years later when I had the opportunity to be present at an event that made the evening news: a protest of abortion in Atlanta. The edited images shown on the news gave an impression very different from the reality: that the pro-life and

---

[77] George Orwell, *1984* (1949; NY: New American Library, 1961): 245.

pro-choice contingents were equal in size for example, when the pro-lifers actually outnumbered their opponents ten to one. But where was the reality? Inside the heads of a few thousand people who would only be around for a new more decades. And where was the edited image? In the heads of hundreds of thousands who had seen the news, and archived to be replayed until the collapse of the civilization that had made such recordings possible. Parts at least of Orwell's dystopian vision had become technically possible. If truth is nothing more than a subjective memory, it is helpless against the image that replaces it.

Tolkien in fact would help me survive that crisis, restoring an emotional stability and (along with his friend C. S. Lewis) giving me an intellectual rootedness in the solidity of the most important truths. "How shall a man judge what to do in such times," Eomer will ask later. "As he has ever done," Aragorn will reply. "Good and ill have not changed since yesteryear, nor are they one thing among Elves and Dwarves and another among Men."[78] Aragorn is able to say this because Iluvatar exists; Iluvartar knows; and Iluvatar remains. If he doesn't—if truth has no grounding beyond individual subjectivity—we are of all men most miserable.

Reading *1984* to set up *The Lord of the Rings* has always seemed to me a crucial part of my education. It happened that way by chance, if chance you call it. If you have young people to educate, making it happen deliberately would be no bad thing.

The fall of Gandalf was less depressing but much more sorrowful. I was weeping right along with Frodo and Sam on our way out through the Gate. It was a necessary sacrifice, both dramatically and thematically. But what a sacrifice! And today, even though I now have been reminded more than fifty times that he is coming back, it was the summer of '68 all over again.

---

[78] Tolkien, *The Two Towers*, op. cit., 48.

Fifty-seven years later, I have still not found two more devastating moments in literature. I hope I never will.

## DAY 39

# The Fellowship of the Ring
## *"Lothlorien"*

"Lothlorien" is the chapter that needs to follow "The Bridge of Khazad-Dum." In no place else could the needed peace and healing be found. Frodo will give us an excellent poetic elegy for Gandalf in the next chapter. Here as we enter the peace of the yellow Wood, I am moved to utter my own, using the same form, for Gandalf's creator:

> To J. R. R. Tolkien
> On a day when Fall's first leaves were flying
> And the wind was howling and geese were crying
> And clouds were black and the sun was hiding,
> Word first came, on dark wings riding.
> > "Tolkien is dead,"
> > Was all they said,
> > And left us crying.
>
> He heard by light of star and moon
> The Elven songs and learned their tunes.
> He had long walks with them, and talks,
> Beneath the swaying trees in June.
>
> Dwarf-mines deeply delved he saw
> Where Mithril glittered on the walls

And mighty kings wrought wondrous things
And reigned in hollow, torch-lit halls.

To forests wild and deep he went
And many lives of men he spent
Where leaves of years fall soft like tears,
Listening to the speech of Ents.

In lofty halls of men he sat
Or rustic rooms of bar-man fat;
In hobbit holes, heard stories told
By an old man in a wizard's hat.

With magic words of dark and light
And days of doom and coming night
And magic rings and hoped for spring,
He wrought the record of his sight....

In Beowulf's bold fleet he sailed,
With Gawain the Green Knight beheld;
By Beortnoth's side he stood and cried
And hordes of pagan Danes he felled,
"Will shall be sterner, heart the bolder,
Spirit the greater as our strength fails!'

On a day when Fall's first leaves were flying
And the wind was howling and geese were crying
And clouds were black and the sun was hiding,
Word first came, on dark wings riding.
    "Tolkien is dead,"
    Was all they said,
    And left us crying.[79]

And where else can one possibly find such wisdom as we find in such a minor character as Haldir?

---

[79] *Stars through the Clouds*, op. cit., 353.

"I am not the master of the law and cannot set it aside."[80]

"In nothing is the power of the Dark Lord more clearly seen than in the estrangement that divides all who still oppose him."[81]

"The world is indeed full of peril, and in it there are many dark places; but sill there is much that is fair, and though in all lands love is now mingled with grief, it grows perhaps the greater."[82]

Yes.

---

[80] FOTR, op. cit., 411.

[81] Ibid.

[82] Ibid., 412.

## DAY 40

# The Fellowship of the Ring
### *"The Mirror of Galadriel" and*
### *"Farewell to Lorien"*

"The Mirror of Galadriel" and "Farewell to Lorien" are chapters in which it seems at first that not much is happening. But in the first place, not much needs to happen. It is enough just to be in Loth Lorien, not as homelike as Rivendell but a haunting memory of something Edenic whose illusion of timelessness is not quite enough to avoid the hints that its days are numbered. In the second place, it turns out that some pretty significant things do happen: Frodo and Sam's visions in the Mirror of Galadriel turn into a test for their hostess as well as for them, and the foundation is laid for Gimli's devotion to Galadriel and friendship with Legolas.

Galadriel has learned a lot since she was a hot-headed Elf Maiden in the train of Feanor. She was an eyewitness to the effect the Silmaril had on Thingol, and she has had plenty of time to think about it. Her refusal of the Ring is the fruit of that meditation. So is her wisdom in general. She warns Sam that some of the visions in her mirror "never come to be unless those who behold the vision turn aside from their path to prevent them."[83] The irony in that observation will be fully incarnated in a future age by Oe-

---

[83] Ibid., 428.

dipus, who is warned by the oracle of Apollo that he will kill his father and marry his mother, Not realizing that he has been adopted, he runs away from home to make sure this never happens, only to meet and kill his birth father on that very journey in a dispute over the right of way. He then proceeds into Thebes, defeats the Sphinx who is plaguing the city, and, as the king has inexplicably disappeared, is hailed as the new king and married to the reigning queen—his birth mother. Readers of Sophocles's play will find in its plot a powerful commentary on Galadriel's warning.

Galadriel also gives us one of the most hauntingly beautiful songs in the canon, "I sang of leaves, of leaves of gold, and leaves of gold there grew." It was haunting when we did not really know what she was talking about, and no less so now that her backstory in *The Silmarillion* and her involvement in Feanor's rebellion explain the final question about that ship.

Speaking of beauty, Gimli's concept of it, founded in the carven stone and wroughten metal of the Dwarvish heart, deepens and blossoms through Galadriel's inspiration into one of the finest expressions of Lewis's *sehnsucht* ever spoken:

> "Tell me, Legolas, why did I come on this quest? Little did I know where the chief peril lay.... . Torment in the dark was the danger that I feared, and it did not hold me back. But I would not have come had I known the danger of light and joy. Now I have taken my worst wound in this parting, even if I were to go this night straight to the Dark Lord. Alas for Gimli son of Gloin!"[84]

Nay, alas for us all, for in this Middle-earth parting and memory is all we are finally left with, unless Aragorn's hope be true that beyond the circles of the world there is more than memory. Until then, may our memories be as poignant, and as clear and unstained, as Gimli's.

[84] Ibid., 446.

## DAY 41

# The Fellowship of the Ring

### "The Great River" and "The Breaking of the Fellowship"

Tolkien says he never planned for *The Lord of the Rings* to be a trilogy. It came out in three volumes as an accident of publication because it was just too big to be held by one cover. But *The Fellowship of the Ring* could not have ended at a more effective place with a more harrowing cliffhanger if it had been planned that way. With Frodo and Sam secretly lighting out for Mordor and the rest of the Company in chaos, we can hardly pause for a deep breath before opening volume two the first time through. Fifty-plus times after that, we have leisure to pause and think about what is happening.

Boromir is corrupted by the Ring after having had only one brief glimpse of it and never actually touching it. And he was ostensibly the noblest product of the noblest human culture then present in Middle-earth. (Faramir is the character who actually fits that description, but Boromir should have done.) We see that this is no protection. Elrond and Gandalf had not exaggerated the Ring's seductive power. Frodo is protected, for now, by that fact that Ring-bearer is his calling and by the warning of his heart against three things: the easy way out, refusal of the burden, and trust in the strength and truth of men. Boromir was not chosen, and his heart fatally does trust in the strength and truth of men. Still, we are impressed by how easily he falls, and we should be even more impressed by contrast with Frodo's achievement of staving off that corruption to the bitter end before even he is overwhelmed at Sammath Naur. That profound passage will be dealt with in due time, but we see here that Tolkien's labors to set it up are unceasing.

The mystery of how human choices somehow work together with fate to enact destiny without being reduced to a mechanical determinism has taxed the greatest human thinkers from Sophocles to St. Paul to Calvin and beyond. None of them can explain the mystery; they can only try to capture it. Tolkien does so with his characteristic mastery. Frodo on Amon Hen is caught between the Eye demanding his surrender and the Voice (which turns out to be Gandalf's) crying, "Take it off! Fool! Take off the Ring!"

"The two powers strove in him. For a moment, perfectly balanced between their piercing points, he writhed, tormented. Suddenly he was aware of himself again, Frodo, neither the Voice nor the Eye, free to choose, and with one remaining instant in which to do so. He took off the Ring."[85]

How does Frodo make that choice? We only know that he can, because at times we have done so too. And at times we have failed to do so, and we can no more explain the difference between those times than any of the sages who came before us. When Frodo can no longer make that choice, well … that is almost two volumes away, and it will call forth perhaps the greatest eucatastrophic irony in all of literature. We will save it for when we get there. Sufficient unto the volume is the mystery thereof.

But for now, we cross the river. What must come will come.

---

[85] Ibid., 472.

# DAY 42
# The Two Towers
### "The Departure of Boromir" and
### "The Riders of Rohan"

Frodo and Sam we last saw heading off across the waste toward Mordor. It will be half a volume before we return to them. It is a testament to Tolkien's skill that in the meantime we are totally absorbed by what even Aragorn himself calls "a small matter in the great deeds of our time" by comparison. But Aragorn was not completely right about that. Without the contributions of each surviving member of the Fellowship, as we will discover, Frodo and Sam could not have succeeded. Once we have seen that, watching Tolkien set it up in subsequent readings is a lesson in good story structure.

The story structure being used is called *interlacement*, where several parallel storylines are kept going simultaneously. Here we have the Frodo-and-Sam narrative, the Aragorn-Legolas-and-Gimli narrative, and the Merry-and-Pippin narrative being interlaced. Each thread is being played out with the characters ignorant of what is happening in the others, while the reader switches back and forth between them. It keeps arousing and satisfying curiosity, arousing and allaying suspense on the part of the reader. Tolkien will also use it to reinforce his theme of the necessity of walking by faith and not by sight if we are to be faithful in Arda marred. The reader begins to see what the characters cannot see, knowing only their own threads as they do. As Shippey puts it, it creates an "anti-irony": "One slowly realizes that the characters' frustration, gloom, even approach to despair, is at once natural and justified, and also needless and falsified."[86] The reader sees what the characters must take on trust: that their actions are not pointless or in vain. We will see many ways in which this works itself out as we proceed.

Meanwhile, in the first couple of chapters, Boromir gets a ship burial that would have made the *Beowulf* poet proud, we start to find out who belongs on the medal stand for the triathlon in the Middle-earth Olympics, and we first encounter the Rohirrim—the culture of the Geats and the Spear-Danes from *Beowulf* with horses thrown in.

Eomer's education, his introduction to a larger world, gets kick-started in a way that had to be somewhat disorienting for him, but which occasioned two of the great exchanges in all of literature. What, Eomer wants to know, halflings are not just a myth? "Do we walk in legends or on the green earth in the daylight?" "A man may do both," Aragorn replies. "The green earth, say you? That is a mighty matter of legend, though you tread it under the light of day."[87] And so it is, if we but stop to notice. Thus Tolkien works to undo the disenchantment of the world that has been the result of a mindlessly accepted modernity.

The other exchange also works to undo the damage modernity (and now Post-Modernity) has done to our very humanity. "How shall a man judge what to do in such times?" Eomer asks. "As he has ever done," said Aragorn. "Good and ill have not changed since yesteryear, nor are they one thing among Elves

---

[86] *Author of the Century*, op. cit., 110.
[87] *The Two Towers*, op. cit., 43–4.

and Dwarves and another among Men."[88] The opposite idea does not really need to be refuted, for it refutes itself if once we stop to think about it. Tolkien gives us the opportunity to do that, to realize that another perspective is possible.

Good and ill had not changed for Eomer and Aragorn. Nor have they changed or become some other thing as deeply into the Fourth Age as we are, you and I. I think they still might last a while yet.

---

[88] Ibid., 48.

# DAY 43

# The Two Towers

## *"The Uruk Hai" and "Treebeard"*

Merry and Pippin's forced march with the Orcs is a nightmare, but a necessary nightmare which serves to introduce them to Treebeard. Thus Saruman gets to participate in what Eru had warned would be the fate of all who oppose his Music: A being who attempts this will not be able to alter it in Iluvatar's despite, but will only prove his "instrument in the devising of things more wonderful, which he himself hath not imagined."[89] If Morgoth was unable to escape this fate, and we see it being played out in the case of Saruman's desire to capture the Hobbits, we can surely hope that Sauron will not be able to prove an exception either.

We get here the clearest portrait of Orc nature and culture that we will see until we reach Cirith Ungol. Perhaps it is the time to mention the biggest controversy about the Orcs. Has Tolkien created an irredeemable race, and was it right for him to do so, especially given that the Orcs have Elvish ancestry? (They are descended from Elves ruined by Morgoth.) We have no definitive statement about their redeemability; we simply know of no example of an Orc who repents. It is certainly conceivable that in the corruption of an individual or a race there is a point of no

---

[89] *Silmarillion*, op. cit., 17.

return, and it is hardly an ethical problem for Tolkien or his Orc hunters if the Orcs be thought to have reached it. Besides, Tolkien had a precedent in the Christian tradition, where the fallen angels are not offered redemption. It certainly explains why the creation of the Orcs is listed as Morgoth's most evil deed.[90]

The Ents are one of Tolkien's most original creations. Treebeard has C. S. Lewis's voice, by report ("Hrum, hoom!"), but Tolkien's personality—he was one of the greatest lovers of trees and one of the most unhasty people the world has ever seen. I wish I could have heard the roar of laughter in the Inklings meeting when Tollers read the passage where Treebeard refers to the "Old Entish."[91] Tolkien was of course Oxford's Bosworth professor of Anglo-Saxon, or "Old English." What really struck me this time, though, was a comment Treebeard makes about the search for the Entwives:

"We believe that we may meet again in time to come, and perhaps we shall find somewhere a land where we can both live together and be content. But it is foreboded that that will only be when we have both lost all that we now have."[92]

This pattern, ultimate gain that comes only through a seemingly ultimate loss, is a paradigm for life in Arda Marred, and each of the Free Peoples has its own way of experiencing it. The Elves are immortal within the life of the world, but they must still eventually give up Rivendell or Loth Lorien to return to Aman. The Doom of Men makes us face the loss of everything we have built relatively quickly and forces us to cling to Aragorn's hope that beyond the circles of the world is "more than memory"[93]; else we are of all the children of Iluvatar most miserable. Hobbits

[90] Ibid., 50.
[91] *Two Towers*, op. cit., 80.
[92] Ibid., 94.
[93] "The Tale of Aragorn and Arwen," *ROTK*, op. cit., Appendices, 389.

are a sub-species of man. Sam gets to enjoy the Shire for a long life, but even he will eventually have to say farewell to Rosie. As the Ringbearer, Frodo is forced to face this truth more quickly. He understands that often someone has to give things up so that others may keep them. The Shire was saved, but not for him,[94] so he has to set sail from the Havens to seek healing. His wounds simply strip away the veil and make him face more immediately what is ultimately true for everyone; They strip away his illusions but not his hope. Treebeard's foreboding turns out to be more thematically important than we may realize at the time.

In the meantime, Saruman is in serious trouble.

---

[94] Ibid., 345.

# The Two Towers
## *"The White Rider" and 'The King of the Golden Hall"*

To tell you the truth, on my first reading I had mixed emotions about Gandalf's return. I was happy to see him, but part of me felt that it had somehow cheapened his sacrifice on the Bridge of Khazad-Dum. Now that I know he is a Maia and understand more about the nature of wizards and their mission, his being "sent back" by the Valar makes perfectly good sense. But I wonder if anyone else had the same reaction back in the old days before we knew what *The Silmarillion* has to teach us.

In any case, Tolkien is wisely careful to have Christ analogs without creating Christ figures. Being a Christ figure is a burden greater than almost any believable fictional character can bear. C. S. Lewis's Lion Aslan is the exception that proves the rule, and he only just pulls it off by being the King of Beasts, not a man. Tolkien wasn't so sure that Aslan does pull it off, and he tells us plainly that he himself would not have dared to try. "The incarnation of God is an *infinitely* greater thing than anything I would dare to write."[95] We can admire his humility and understand and

---

[95] *Letters*, op. cit., 237; emphasis in the original.

appreciate his own approach without adopting his view of Narnia—which has been exaggerated in any case.[96]

Tolkien avoids the problem by dividing the functions of Christ's traditional three offices among different characters. Gandalf reminds us of Christ the Prophet as Aragorn reminds us of Christ the King and Frodo Christ the sacrificial Priest. But none of them is *too* close. They can thus remind us of the greater Hero they resemble, and which resemblance is a key to their own greatness, without any one of them having to bear the impossible burden of being believable as the whole package. Gandalf's return reminds us of Christ's, but it is different from Christ's resurrection: Jesus had no need to take time off for healing in Loth Lorien before returning to His disciples. And Gandalf is not elevated to the right hand of Iluvatar's throne because he did not come from there in the first place.

Hama is straight outta *Beowulf*, along with Meduseld itself and a great deal of Rohan's culture—though neither the Danes, the Geats, nor the Saxons were a horse-based society in the same way as the Rohirrim. Morphing the Anglo-Saxons with the Mongol hordes makes for a pretty powerful people, once their king is healed and re-engaged. (*Theoden* is after all simply the Anglo-Saxon world for king; *Meduseld* is Anglo-Saxon for mead hall; and the beat goes on.) Peter Jackson turns Tolkien's wake-up call into a less believable exorcism while "youthening" Theoden way too much—he should still be an old man, not Jackson's suddenly middle-aged king. Tolkien, by contrast, makes the story so believable you have to remind yourself that it is fantasy.

Wait, did I actually just say that? It is *history*, and Tolkien merely the translator of *The Red Book of Westmarch*. I'm going to go wash my mouth out with soap now.

---

[96] For a balanced treatment, see Williams, *An Encouraging Thought*, op. cit., 112–29.

# DAY 45

# The Two Towers

## *"Helm's Deep" and "The Road to Isengard"*

We meet the Huorns in the chapter "Helm's Deep" and realize what they are in "The Road to Isengard." With all his skill at special effects, Peter Jackson's leaving them out of the battle was a major disappointment. They and their Entish shepherds bring to mind one of my favorite stories about Tolkien.

When he first read "Macbeth" as a young boy, Ronald got really excited at the prophecy that Macbeth could not be defeated "until Birnam Wood do come to Dunsinane." Then, when the fulfillment was just Malcolm's army cutting off branches in the wood and carrying them to hide their numbers, he was horribly let down and swore that one day he would write that scene properly. And this oath was fulfilled in the attack of the Ents on Isengard and the arrival of the Huorns at Helm's Deep. True story—and almost as good as the one we that resulted from it! Many of us have been inspired by Shakespeare, but never quite like that. Well played, Will—and Ronald.

Meanwhile, Merry and Pippin have grown, and not just from drinking Ent Draught. Their reintroduction to the main narrative is one of the most satisfying scenes in the book, skillfully blending comic relief with matters most serious. One of those matters is the theme of friendship. From the friendship between Gandalf and Bilbo and then Frodo, the deepening bond between Frodo and Sam, the wonderful conspiracy of the four friends revealed at Crickhollow, the touching relationship that develops between Merry and Pippin and Treebeard, and the strong inter-species bond that has grown between Aragorn, Legolas, and Gimli, the importance and the power for good of simple male friendship (no intrusive homoeroticism needed) has been one of the driving motifs of the story. We are reminded of its centrality here both by the reunion of the Hobbits with their friends and by the beginning of the strange and heartwarming relationship that will develop between Merry and Theoden. One of the saddest things about Saruman's (and Sauron's) minds of metal and gears, and one of the chief reasons never to believe their lies and be seduced into following them, is their complete inability to appreciate, or even understand, that.

A side note: One of the rare occasions where Tolkien left some confusing inconsistencies in the text is Gandalf's statement to Theoden that when he speaks with Treebeard he will be conversing with "the oldest of all living things."[97] We may remember that Tom Bombadil also claims to be "eldest," and to have been in Middle-earth before the trees which the Ents shepherd.[98] Well, we can chalk this up to Bombadil's role as an enigma or speculate that he is not a "living creature" like the Children of Iluvatar, the Dwarves, and the Ents: beings created to be incarnate spirits, not creatures created to be spirits who happen to be incarnate. If Tom is a Maia or a Vala (or something else altogether—nobody knows for sure), he is in a different category from Treebeard and both may be the oldest in their own weight classification, as it were. But what of Treebeard's statement that there are dales in

[97] *Two Towers*, op. cit., 193.
[98] *FOTR*, op. cit.,

which the trees are older than he is?[99] Certainly trees are living things. Gandalf may have meant Treebeard was the oldest *sentient* creature—but that is not what he said. No doubt he could explain himself better if he had time.

---

[99] *Two Towers*, op. cit., 84.

# DAY 46

# The Two Towers

## *"Flotsam and Jetsam" and "The Voice of Saruman"*

Merry, Pippin, Aragorn, Legolas, and Gimli have a lot of catching up to do, and it is so important that we have a whole chapter to let them do it while everyone else is doing what would seem to be the more urgent and pressing debriefing with Gandalf and Treebeard. Once again the importance of the theme of friendship is brought home. One thinks of the role of the Inklings in Tolkien's life, and before that the Tea Club and Barovian Society. Losing most of your close friends in The Great War would certainly burn the value of friendship into your soul. We have to conclude that Tolkien's circle did not die in vain. Their grand schemes for the benefit of the world[100] were not in fact destroyed by the War; they came to fruition in the pages of *The Lord of the Rings*, where simply reveling in the goodness of friendship is one of the most powerful reminders that there is good in the world that is worth fighting for (even if Sam does only say that in the Movie). Also, the importance of the seemingly small and weak comes once again to the fore. Aragorn learns of the presence of Southfarthing Leaf in Isengard and decides to take it up with Gandalf, as small

---

[100]Tolkien thought that the TCBS had been "granted some spark of fire ... that was destined to kindle a new light, or, what is the same thing, to rekindle an old light in the world; that the TCBS was destined to testify for God and truth." *Letters*, op. cit., 10. Cf. Carpenter, *Tolkien: A Biography* (Boston: Houghton Mifflin, 1977): 73.

a thing as it might seem. We will find out when we get back to the Shire that it was no small matter after all.

"The Voice of Saruman" is a brilliant analysis-by-portrait of a certain kind of corruption of human rhetoric that requires no literal magic to pull off.

> Those who listened unwarily to that voice could seldom report the words that they had heard, and if they did, they wondered, for little power remained in them. Mostly they remembered only that it was a delight to hear the voice speaking, all that it said seemed wise and reasonable, and desire awoke in them by swift agreement to seem wise themselves.[101]

We watch Saruman practicing his art with a disturbing feeling of having heard something like it before. In rhetorical terms it is all *pathos* (appeal to emotion), unfounded in any adequate basis of *ethos* (character) or *logos* (rational content). And the results can be evil indeed.

When people are ignorant of or unpracticed in the skills of critical thinking, they become particularly susceptible to this kind of manipulation. Saruman's skill enhanced by magic created a performance that even the Wise had consciously to resist. Our educational system, more focused on giving people self-esteem and "safe spaces" than on training people for the rough and tumble of serious debate and sagacious discernment, has given us a populace so lacking in resistance that even moderately accomplished manipulators can have a Saruman-like effect. It is not hard to think of currently or recently popular preachers and politicians who have had followings some of whom sound very much as if they were mesmerized by Saruman's voice. Those politicians appear on both sides of the political aisle. If you pay attention to this chapter, you won't need a Palantir to spot them.

---

[101] *Two Towers*, op. cit., 215–16.

And there are people who think fantasy is not relevant to real life!

# DAY 47

# The Two Towers
## *"The Palantir"*

In a fit of spite, Grima throws a convenient orb at Gandalf and Theoden, and Saruman's reaction shows that, once again, there is something going on behind the scenes that gives the free peoples a fighting chance they otherwise would not have. This has been happening ever since Bilbo arrived at Lake Town by what turned out to be the only way that was any good, funneled there by events that each seemed individually like the worst of luck, but which added up to an outcome not intended by any of the parties to those events. That outcome nevertheless tempts one to think that there is some kind of plan behind it all. We just saw it again with Saruman's orcs succeeding only in arranging the Hobbits' meeting with Treebeard which is the key to Saruman's fall. It sets up more than that, for Aragorn's use of the Palantir will be a key to keeping Sauron's attention away from Frodo and Sam.

In the present instance, Pippin peeks in the Palantir and is saved "by good fortune, *as it is called*," says Gandalf (emphasis added).[102] Virtually every single time *chance* or its sibling words like *luck* or *fortune* are invoked in *The Lord of the Rings* (I would say every time, except if I did, somebody would find the one ex-

---

[102] Ibid., 235.

ception and prove me wrong), it is subtly taken back, by the narrator if not by a character: Variations of "Chance, if chance you call it" occur again and again. The pattern implies that something more than mere chance is at work.

This pattern is brought into the clearest focus Tolkien is willing to give it by Gandalf's famous statement that Bilbo was *meant* to find the Ring, and not by its Maker.[103] This, Gandalf says, is the clearest he can make it. But readers of the entire Legendarium who are capable of putting two and two together can achieve a little more clarity than that. As we learn from *The Silmarillion*, Iluvatar is still at work in the world. And that is an encouraging thought because it means that Gandalf's wisdom really is wisdom and not the supreme folly it seems to Denethor, blinded to everything except what can be seen with the eyes of flesh by his own Palantir working on his hubris. This is a wonderful irony. A Palantir is meant to enhance vision, but its abuse by Denethor (and earlier by Saruman) serves only to blind them to the truth that most needs to be seen and embraced.

Either Gandalf's or Denethor's vision is true. There is no third option, no middle ground. Either Iluvatar is at work and Bilbo was meant to find the Ring and Frodo to have it for a reason, or sending two Tom-fool Hobbits into Mordor with it really is the ultimate folly it seems to those who refuse the faith in Providence which is the basis of Gandalf's wisdom—which is what *makes* it wisdom. So we are reminded once more of the theme of Providence building up to the moment when Gollum, of all people—but that is another scene for another day.

For now, we end the first half of the second volume and get ready to turn back to Frodo and Sam with Gandalf and Pippin riding through the night on Shadowfax as the darkness grows

---

[103] *Fellowship of the Ring*, op, cit., 81.

around them. There is hope that their luck may not run out after all, because things only seem to happen by chance, if chance is what you insist on calling it.

# DAY 48

# The Two Towers

## *"The Taming of Smeagol"*

Frodo is going to Mordor, alone, and Sam is going with him. And that is the way it should be. The other surviving Walkers are swept off by Providence in various necessary directions, but the heart of the quest is here. We are trying as hard as we can to get to the one place we don't want to go to, and Elrond's prophecy of strange help unlooked for is going to be fulfilled. Strange help? Unlooked for? No truer words were uttered since men spoke with mouth!

Gandalf has been telling us all along that Gollum would have a role to play before the end, but who would have guessed it would be like this? That Gollum of all creatures should be the guide that Frodo and Sam trust to bring them safely to Mordor—the irony is rich already, and it is just getting started, building toward a finish that will take our breath away.

In "The Taming of Smeagol," we actually start getting to know the fellow, and it turns out that we already know him very well—all *too* well, in fact. There is a little Gollum in each of us: a wounded child who is a strangely complicated mix of needs, whose selfishness is so pure and simple as to be almost a caricature of innocence, who would betray us in a heartbeat but who also manages to be compellingly human, vulnerable and pitiable.

We have buried him, we have tamed him, we have sophisticated him, or we have tried some combination of the three, but he is still there inside us all. And Tolkien's portrait of his character exposes him. We have the opportunity then to try to figure out how to relate to him, as even Sam and Frodo have to do. We will need all of Frodo's forgiveness and Sam's vigilance, all of Frodo's sternness but none of Sam's anger, if we are to develop a healthy relationship. Whether we do so or not, he is part of our lives for good or for ill.

By letting us see Gollum's conflicts up close along with Frodo's and Sam's reactions to them, Tolkien gives us a view of human nature in its psychological and spiritual depths that is unrivaled. That kind of realistic psychological portraiture is supposed to be the domain of the realistic novel, but this fantasy epic takes us as far in that direction as we are capable of going. That fact is one more index of Tolkien's greatness.

On a more trivial note, Smeagol's name is derived from the Anglo-Saxon verb *smeagan*, which means to ponder, search, or investigate—appropriate for the curiosity he had when he was younger. So it should not be pronounced Smee-gul, as Elijah Woods does in the films. In Anglo-Saxon, two vowels coming together are both individually pronounced, with the stress always on the first one. (This is why, to this day, even after all their mashing up and smoothing out on their long journey to modern English, "When two vowels go walking, / the first does the talking.") So Gollum's proper name should be pronounced more like SMAY-uh-gol, three syllables. If we are going to get to know him, we might as well start there.

# DAY 49
# The Two Towers
### *"The Passage of the Marshes" and*
### *"The Black Gate is Closed"*

If Rivendell and Loth Lorien are as close to Heaven as we are ever likely to get while still in this Middle-earth, the Dead Marshes and the desolation of Gorgoroth (and we might add Saruman's corruption of Isengard) are all the images of Hell we need. It is a testament to Tolkien's skill that he can evoke both so effectively. As an index of how miserable this stage of the journey was, ponder the fact that there was no opportunity for a hot shower and a change of clothes after getting slimed by the Marshes. They just had to keep going. And ponder the fact that without Gollum's treachery—his *treachery*, not just his guidance—Frodo would have walked right up to the Black Gate and been captured, with Sauron surely recovering the Ring and bringing a darkness no end to which could be foreseen. The Sub-Creator works in mysterious ways, his plot-twists to perform.

Gollum gives us an endlessly fascinating picture of evil and its effects on one who has yielded to it: Despite his age, he has all the childishness without the childlikeness of youth. He has existed but not grown; rather, he has lost the curiosity and capacity for wonder inherent in his original name, Smeagol (from

Anglo-Saxon *smeagan*, to think, ponder, investigate). Sam recites poetry about Oliphaunts and gets to see one "to his astonishment and terror and lasting delight."[104] Gollum not only doesn't want to see one. It is worse than that: he "doesn't want them to be."[105] Evil might seem at first like a way of reaching out for something perceived as good, but it is ultimately a rejection of being and incompatible with one's own being and one's own life, as St. Augustine taught us so well.

Maybe this contrast helps explain why we see almost everything in this section through the eyes of Sam. Gollum's mind is shrunken to the size of the Ring, and Frodo's is increasingly preoccupied with the burden of the Ring. Sam's mind, on the other hand, is in a better place: It is actively trying to support and protect Frodo and to pay attention to what is happening in order to figure things out to that end, and it still has room for wonder at the prodigious marvel of an Oliphaunt. Sam is not stupid, but neither is he a towering intellect. He does not need to be. Purpose and openness make his mind a wholesome and useful place essential to the success of the quest, without even the intelligence and learning of Frodo. Mere intelligence without a purpose based on love and friendship reduces pretty quickly to gears and metal, and mere intelligence without a capacity for wonder reduces pretty quickly to ugly and self-centered cynicism. Sam's mind has no room for any of that. It is, therefore, not a bad place from which to view the world at all.

---

[104] *Two Towers*, op. cit., 318.
[105] Ibid., 300.

# DAY 50

# The Two Towers

## *"Of Herbs and Stewed Rabbit" and "The Window on the West"*

"The Window on the West" is a clever chapter title. Not only is Henneth Annun literally a window looking out through the waterfall to the West (like Dry Falls in the mountains of North Carolina, if you have ever been there), but it is the place where we learn more about the True West than has yet been revealed outside of the Appendices and *The Silmarillion*.

One of those revelations is our only glimpse of Numenorean worship in the Trilogy. Faramir and his men have a moment of silence looking West "to Numenor that was, and to Elvenhome that is, and to that which is beyond Elvenhome and will ever be."[106] In the Trilogy, the Valar are mentioned only in passing (may they turn the Mumak of Harad aside!), Iluvatar's (God's) name never appears, and this is the only hint that there is any formal acknowledgement of those realities by any of the free peoples. Why so little? Tolkien said in a famous letter that *The Lord of the Rings* was a "fundamentally religious" work, but that the religious element was "absorbed into the story."[107] In practice this is

---

[106] Ibid., 336.
[107] *Letters*, op. cit., 172.

a good thing. If there were a Church of Iluvatar, it would have to be described, and it would inevitably look either Catholic or Protestant, High-Church, Middle, or Low. Either way, a good portion of Christendom would find itself on the outside looking in, and the universal appeal to mere Christians would be compromised. (The absence of a Church of Aslan is likewise fortunate in C. S. Lewis's Narnia books.) I don't think that was Tolkien's motive, for he was a devout Roman Catholic and to him the work was "fundamentally religious *and Catholic*" (emphasis added).[108] But it was providentially the right decision, in my view, letting the fundamentally Christian elements come through without any sectarian spin. So let's just say it was good luck, if luck you call it.[109]

Then we have Tolkien's own favorite character, Faramir. If you have only seen the movies, know that the Faramir you met there is unrecognizable as the character from the book. How do you get from "I would not take this thing if it lay by the highway"[110] to "Tell my father I send him a powerful weapon"? You get there by not understanding either Tolkien's Christianity or his philosophy of literature. In short, Peter Jackson cannot understand a character with the virtue and integrity Tolkien portrayed in Faramir (or Aragorn, or Arwen, for that matter), so he feels obligated to "complicate" them in the interests of (what is to him) believability. Tolkien thought it more important to give us pictures of what showing "your quality, the very highest" (as Sam would put it) looks like.[111] The difference in philosophical outlook goes a long way toward explaining many of the disparities between book and film.[112]

---

[108] Ibid.

[109] For more on what those Christian elements are, see my earlier book *An Encouraging Thought: The Christian Worldview in the Writings of J. R. R. Tolkien* (Christian Publishing House, 2018).

[110] Two Towers, op. cit., 320.

[111] Ibid., 343.

[112] For a detailed explanation of the differences, see once again *An Encouraging Thought*, op. cit., 70–89.

# DAY 51

# The Two Towers

## "The Forbidden Pool" and "Journey to the Crossroads"

"The fish of this pool are dearly bought." "Don't want fish!"[113] Gollum says whatever appears to him to be advantageous at the moment—like certain public figures we could mention. Words for him are purely instrumental, tools for achieving immediate goals (fish, survival), not servants of Truth. And he is speaking to a man who would not snare an orc with a falsehood! Meanwhile, the seeming "treachery" Frodo must use to save him is an indicator of the moral seriousness of this fantasy work. Life operates in a context of moral absolutes (not changing from yesteryear or differing for Men, Elves, or Dwarves), but this moral clarity does not always provide us with easy answers. Sometimes seemingly intolerable compromises seem unavoidable. We can neither refuse them nor be comfortable with them. The pure joy of the Field of Cormallen is real and something we legitimately hope the universe will support—but sometimes, on the way there, doing the right thing, at least the necessary thing, leaves us feeling wretched. Tolkien's greatness is shown by his holding out the hope of a real moral victory while acknowledging the reality of the wretchedness.

---

[113] *Two Towers*, op. cit., 351.

Once we leave Henneth Annun with our packs newly stocked with provisions, things begin to get seriously dark, both literally and figuratively. Yet at the Crossroads, the sunlight breaks through just long enough to illuminate the crown of flowers Nature had restored to the ruined head of the stone king. The brief glimpse is soon gone, but not before Frodo realizes that "They cannot conquer forever!"[114] Sam will get a similar message later from a star that peeks through the gloom.

Tolkien has taken the Augustinian doctrine of evil as a parasite on the good and embodied it in physical images. The king's flowery crown and Sam's piercing star both testify to the reality that Sauron can only corrupt or obscure for a while a good world that was there before he came and will remain after he is gone. His reeks and smokes cannot really rise above the atmosphere to blot out the sun or extinguish the stars because Iluvatar is the One and no music can be played in His despite. Iluvatar was there before the Ainur, including Sauron's master, Morgoth.

It must be so. Good is creative; evil destructive. Good builds; evil tears down. Good sustains; evil dissipates. Good is wholesome; evil corrupting. Good must be prior both logically and temporally because evil could never create a world; it can only destroy. Light then must remain despite all Sauron can do, though for long stretches until Iluvatar brings about the resolution of the Final Chord we may have to walk by faith in that reality and not by any sight of it at all.

Sam and Frodo need frequently to be reminded of this truth. And so do we.

---

[114] Ibid., 367.

# DAY 52
# The Two Towers
## *"The Stairs of Cirith Ungol" and "Shelob's Lair"*

Frodo and Sam learn some wisdom about stories from thinking about the one they are living. True heroism does not presuppose grand character traits in advance. It is made out of small decisions with big consequences made by ordinary people who just landed in their stories: "those as just went on."[115] The great tales go on and on like the Road in the poem, down from the door where they began. The characters come and go. Their parts, at least, have a beginning and an end. And whether then? The glimpse of that—s glimpse is all we will get—is still a volume away.

One of the saddest scenes in all of literature is Gollum having second thoughts about sending Frodo to death by Shelob, almost repenting, only to be interrupted by Sam as he reaches out to Frodo in what may be the worst timing ever. The moment is lost, never to be recovered. You cannot blame Sam, but what a tragedy that lost moment is! As shrunken as Gollum has become, a shred of potentially recoverable humanity still lurks within him. But it has to be chosen to be recovered, and a lifetime of slavery to the Ring makes that choosing no simple matter.

Yet where could the story have gone had that impulse toward repentance on Gollum's part been allowed to play out?

---

[115] Ibid., 378.

Would either he or Frodo have been able to maintain that new relationship when they got to Sammath Naur? Would Iluvatar have come up with some other unexpected act of Providence, no more predictable than the one we will see there, but equally inevitable once it was revealed, to salvage the quest? We will never know.[116] But we see the thin thread on which fate sometimes hangs put on display in a manner that takes our breath away. There but for the grace of God ...

We did not know what the name Cirith Ungol meant until we could read *The Silmarillion*. But even without being able to get the allusion to Shelob's horrid ancestor Ungoliant, we could see another brilliant picture of evil through the eyes of Augustine: the self *incurvatus in se*, curved (or bent, or maybe even better, warped) in upon itself. Gollum almost reaches out to Frodo in what is almost a caress before tragically pulling back in—*incurvatus in se*. Ungoliant and Shelob are never even tempted to reach outward in love. They do not even have the sorry excuse of rebellion against Iluvatar to motivate their twisted lives. They just want to absorb all other life until they finally devour themselves. Our own selfishness, our own self-centeredness, our own temptations to make life self-referential, are pitiful shadows of that darkness, differing from it in degree only, not in kind. Let us turn from all of that before Galadriel's light becomes a piercing pain to us in our own self-imposed darkness.

---

[116] Though Tolkien had thought about it and had some very interesting speculations. *Letters*, op. cit., 330.

# The Two Towers

## *"The Choices of Master Samwise"*

When it was Frodo's turn to make a seemingly impossible choice, at Amon Hen, we commented as follows:

> The mystery of how human choices somehow work together with fate to enact destiny without being reduced to a mechanical determinism has taxed the greatest human thinkers from Sophocles to St. Paul to Calvin and beyond. None of them can explain the mystery; they can only try to capture it. Tolkien does so with his characteristic mastery (p. 119).

Caught between the Eye and the Voice, Frodo has a moment where he is himself and able to choose. He takes off the Ring and survives with his integrity intact to pursue the next phase of the quest. Sam's dilemma is different, if not equally difficult, but it partakes of the same mystery. He is not poised between two external wills competing for dominance but between alternatives that nothing in his nature has prepared him to deal with. What is that nature? Sam completely inhabits the identity of a servant. Everything in him is committed to supporting Mr. Frodo in his mission, no matter what the cost.

Sam has all the integrity an individual can have, but it is integrity in those terms. It is sufficient to help him reject the mindless pursuit of Gollum for vengeance. That he might still do at some point, but it was not what he came for; it would justify leaving his master. Suicide is also rejected. It is to make no choice at all, certainly not one consistent with faithfulness to his master. It does not serve Mr. Frodo in any way. To take the Ring and continue the quest himself? To be himself the Ring Bearer, the master and not the servant? It is clear that, given that Sam thinks Frodo is dead, this is the right choice because of the stakes and because it is what Frodo would have wanted based on his own commitment to the mission. Sam is capable of reasoning this out. And he makes that choice. But we do not understand Samwise Gamgee unless we understand the cost of that choice to him, as high as any cost paid by any character in the book.

Sam makes the choice, but it is so contrary to his every instinct that he cannot make it completely. When Frodo's body is taken he turns back in spite of himself. It is an understandable unchoosing, but it is wrong. Would Frodo have cared more about what happens to his body than the success of the quest? Surely not. But once again we sense a higher power at work, using Sam's weakness *and* his integrity as well as Frodo's so that we will end up coming to Sammath Naur, as we did to the Lonely Mountain, by the only road that was finally any good. For Frodo is not dead after all, only paralyzed, and so between Sam's head, his instincts, and his heart, he ironically makes what turns out to be the right choice after all.

Can Tolkien write a cliff-hanger or what? Frodo was alive but taken by the enemy. For the reader, getting *The Two Towers* back in the slipcover and pulling out *The Return of the King* is an act of desperation.

# DAY 54
# The Return of the King
## *"Minas Tirith"*

I almost wish Gondor still existed so I could swear the oath of fealty. Doing it with Pippin stirs the blood with patriotism and with hunger for a nation that could deserve it. Our (American) pledge of allegiance promises less, but makes appropriate promises to a Republic, which we were given, as Benjamin Franklin said to an enquirer after the Constitutional Convention, "If you can keep it." Gondor did not keep the monarchy it was given, but they will get it back for a while, if they can keep it. In the long run, nobody ever does. That is why we wait for the King to return, whether Aragorn or Arthur or one greater still. And I say, the sooner the better.

Speaking of not having kept the monarchy, Denethor, the Steward of Gondor, almost rivals Faramir as the most unrecognizable character in the Peter Jackson films: interesting, as they are not exactly unrelated. Denethor as Tolkien wrote him is a classical tragic hero whose real nobility is undermined by his hubris; Denethor as Jackson transformed him is merely a dottering old idiot. One just wants to look away from both of them, but for very different reasons. The tension between Denethor and Gandalf in the book is important thematically as well as dramatically.

Both of them are stewards, but only one remembers what that means. A stewardship, if you can keep it.

The most striking passage for me in "Minas Tirith" is Pippin looking past the lines of care in Gandalf's face to become aware of the fountain of mirth underneath, enough to set a kingdom laughing.[117] I know of only one figure in literature or history who has the same combination of traits in even more intense abundance. Christ is also a "man of sorrows and acquainted with grief" (Is 53.3) who is the source of "joy unspeakable and full of glory" (1 Pet 1.8). We have already discussed the fact that Tolkien does not have "Christ figures" as such, but he does have characters who remind us of certain traits of that greater Hero in ways that are not accidental. They include Gandalf as Christ the prophet, Frodo as Christ the priest, and Aragorn as Christ the king, dividing up the traditional Offices so that nobody has to bear the unbearable burden and all can believable. Here Gandalf reminds us of Christ more potently than at perhaps any other moment since his return as the White Rider. Gandalf is a servant of the Secret Fire; Christ is *the* Servant promised by Isaiah (chp. 53). Neither has forgotten his stewardship.

Sorrow and joy, together, just like this: If you can believe in Christ, as Gandalf (and Frodo and Aragorn) help us understand Him, you have to follow Him. And that is all there is to say about that.

---

[117] ROTK, op. cit., 33.

# DAY 55
# The Return of the King
## *"The Passing of the Grey Company"*

For a man fully committed to the traditional family and traditional gender roles, and writing in the 1940s, Tolkien shows in his development of Eowyn's character a remarkable understanding of the frustrations that fueled the feminist movements of the1950s and beyond. She is not content to be burned in the house after the men have no further need of it. And why should she be? Yet in Aragorn, Tolkien offers no compromise with some of the conclusions secular feminism would unfortunately come to. Many will not agree, but I think that is just the combination we still need today. Perhaps, had there been more men capable of such understanding and sympathy, the movement might have been healthier and certain segments of it less destructive. Maybe we could have given women more freedom and choices without sometimes seeming to devalue their traditional roles. Meanwhile, Eowyn is not allowed to escape her duty, but she is granted to express her fear: a cage. Such is not what awaits her.[118]

In any case, Aragorn's loyalty to Arwen (and hers to him) in the book is as inspiring as it is sadly lacking in the films, where Aragorn actually thinks of Eowyn as a possibility, and Arwen ac-

---

[118] Ibid., 62.

tually heads off to the Havens before thinking better of it. Elrond too in the book is truly one of the Wise, willing to make the bitter sacrifice but only if it is truly providentially asked of him: Arwen may wed only a mortal man who is king of the restored and re-united Numenorean realms of Gondor and Arnor. In the movies, he acts from selfish motives. That was not the sage of Rivendell; that was not the King of Men; that was not the Evenstar of her people. Praised be Iluvatar that Tolkien gave us better.

Aragorn concludes that he can only make his contribution to the war by taking The Paths of the Dead, a decision that strikes fear and bewilderment into Eowyn and everyone else who hears of it, including some of Aragorn's own company. Why can we not adopt Legolas's attitude to the Paths of the Dead? Everyone is terrified of those ghosts, but they never actually *do* anything to anybody. They are thus the perfect embodiment of C. S. Lewis's description of the numinous in *The Problem of Pain*.[119] Lewis con-templates the difference between the fear that might accompany the belief that there is a man-eating tiger in the next room and that which might accompany the belief that there is a ghost in the next room. The fear, dread, and awe that are independent of any threatened physical damage in the latter case says something about human nature and its capacity for intuiting or experiencing the supernatural. One does not fear the dead so much for what they might do as for what they are. Lewis's discussion thus forms a perfect commentary on the ride of the Grey Company and the courage it required. It is also a wonderfully satisfying irony that the fulfillment of the oath of the dead allows Aragorn to use one of Sauron's chief weapons—unreasoning fear—against him.

---

[119] C. S. Lewis, *The Problem of Pain* (NY: MacMillan, 1967), 4–9.

# DAY 56
# The Return of the King
## *"The Muster of Rohan"*

"The slow, sonorous speech of Rohan" as heard by Merry is a perfect description of the way Old English sounds to an uninitiated modern speaker: "It was a language in which there seemed to be many words that he knew, though spoken more strongly and richly than in The Shire, yet he could not piece the words together."[120] The speech of the Rohirrim, then, is related to Westron as Old English is to Modern English, which reinforces the many cultural parallels between the Rohirrim and the Anglo-Saxons.

To see how perfect the description is, contemplate the following sentence in Old English. *"Faeder ure, thu the eart in heofenum, sy thin nama gehalgod."* If you remember your Early Modern (King-James, Shakespearean) English, every word but one should be familiar to you, but the more Germanic sound and syntax keeps most people from recognizing it until after they are told, at which point it becomes obvious. It is the first line of The Lord's Prayer: "Our Father who art in Heavan, hallowed by thy name." Yes: Many words that you know, or at least recognize as earlier forms of words you know once you realize what they are, but you might well have needed a little help to piece them together.

---

[120] ROTK, op, cit., 70.

Exactly. Tolkien was not the greatest Philologist of his generation for nothing. (*Never* call Shakespeare or the King-James Bible "Old English," by the way. They are *Early Modern* English!)

The poetry of the Rohirrim, by the way, is Anglo-Saxon Alliterative Meter. To simplify: You have a four-beat line in which the major sound device is not rhyme but alliteration. The third beat is called "the head-stave." It is the key to the alliteration. One of the first two stressed syllables must, and both may, alliterate with it. Thus, "From **dark Dun**harrow in the **dim mor**ning / With **thane** and **cap**tain rode **The**ngel's **son**."[121] That is enough to go on with. If you want detailed instruction in the niceties and the nuances of this form, you can get it fully but succinctly from C. S. Lewis.[122] This was the original meter of *Beowulf* and "Caedmon's Hymn," and Tolkien uses it deftly in his Modern-English translations of the bards of Rohan.

"Where will wants not, a way opens,"[123] says Dernhelm to Merry, as good a stave of alliterative wisdom and as good a summary of "The Muster of Rohan" as we need look to find. And so Merry takes his new gear into the gloom, with little idea that he can do any good with it. But he will not be parted from Theoden; neither will Dernhelm (Eowyn in disguise). The picture of love and loyalty they each give in their own way brings a lump to the throat. Not for the last time!

[121] Ibid., 93.
[122] C.S. Lewis, "The Alliterative Meter," *Selected Literary Essays*, ed. Walter Hooper (Cambridge: Cambridge Univ. Pr., 1969): 15–26.
[123] ROTK, op. cit.,., 84.

# The Return of the King
## *"The Siege of Gondor"*

We've hinted at it before, but it is time to stop and once more explicitly admire Tolkien's incredible skill at interlacement, the technique of keeping multiple plot threads going simultaneously while weaving the readers in and out of them so that they stay maximally suspended (and suspenseful) and minimally confused. Right now we have four groupings: Frodo and Sam, Gandalf and Pippin, Merry and Theoden, and Aragorn with Legolas and Gimli, all in parallel timelines. Cutting back and forth between them lets us have more cliffhangers stacked up all waiting for resolution than we can hardly stand, with each one so riveting that we forget how intolerable it is that the last one is still hanging.

How does this work? We just had Gandalf facing down the Witch King of Angmar at the Gate only to hear the horns blowing us back to Merry and Theoden several days ago so we can follow the Rohirrim up to Minas Tirith to blow them. So we leave Pippin hiding in the shadows desperate to get Gandalf's attention to save Faramir while the Gate is about to be breached, and it will take us a whole chapter now to get back there, and we hate it ... but we love it. This writer can do atmosphere so rich we just want to sit in Bag End or the Prancing

Pony or Rivendell and soak it in (and who cares if anything ever happens), and he can do action and masterfully managed suspense too? Hardly anyone else is that good at either skill, and absolutely no one else is that good at both.

Meanwhile, Denethor is a profound study in the psychology (and pathology) of despair. Gandalf's mission is to give hope to the free peoples. One of the ways he does that is by planting in their minds encouraging thoughts like the notion that Bilbo was meant to find the Ring. Such "meaning" cannot be seen with the eyes; it has to be based on faith in Iluvatar at work behind the scenes. If you can believe in that, then you can take risks like trying to destroy the Ring simply because it is the right thing to do, in spite of every merely pragmatic and utilitarian argument against it. If you cannot believe in it, or if you forget it, overwhelmed by the Palantir working on your hubris and showing you just more of what the eyes can see, so that you begin to walk only by sight and not by faith, then Gandalf's wisdom must seem only a fool's hope. Walk by sight (alone) and not by faith, and despair is unavoidable, no matter how deep your commitments and how strong your will. In fact, as Denethor illustrates, the deeper and stronger they are, the worse our despair will be. Walking by faith that there are truths beyond what the eye can see is not a luxury if you want to be faithful.

Gandalf said earlier that if you have a Ranger with you, it is best to pay attention to him. We can add that if you have a faithful Istari with you it is even more important to pay attention to him. Denethor's tragedy is that he cannot.

# DAY 58

# The Return of the King
## *"The Battle of the Pelennor Fields"*

Ideas have consequences, a great book reminds us.[124] And so do the actions that flow from them. Denethor's despair affects not only himself and Faramir. As we will discover, by keeping Gandalf from the field of battle, it contributed to the death of Theoden. But behind the scenes (in the realm of faith, not sight), we can see that Iluvatar is still at work, using even that tragedy to bring about the defeat of the head of the Nazgul and ultimately the union of Eowyn and Faramir.

It is worth noting that Theoden's faithfulness is rewarded by the fact that he dies completely victorious. He is not defeated (directly) even by the Witch King. He dies from the accident, as it were, of being crushed by Snowmane's fall. Truly there would be no shame in being beaten by such a superior foe, but it is satisfying that Theoden is spared even that indignity. It is a fine bit of laconic understatement when he says he will not now be ashamed to meet his heroic ancestors.[125] Indeed, it is hard to imagine any one of them who would stand higher in the test than he does.

The death of the Witch King is one of the great scenes in all of literature, and it is the second parallel with Macbeth. The

---

[124] Richard M. Weaver, *Ideas Have Consequences* (Chicago: Univ. of Chicago Pr., 1948).
[125] ROTK, op. cit., 129.

first is the Ents' attack on Isengard, in which Tolkien fulfilled his childhood oath to have Birnam Wood come to Dunsinane *properly*. Now we echo MacBeth's confidence in the prophecy that he cannot be slain by any man born of woman. MacDuff reveals at the critical moment that he was from his mother's womb untimely ripped, having come into the world by C-section, not by a normal birth. Eowyn undermines Angmar's confidence by not being a man at all. And Merry the Hobbit is not *exactly* a man either, as he would be quick to point out. His stroke to the undead hamstring of the Witch King brings the head into Eowyn's reach, and there is one less Nazgul to trouble the world.

It is all very exciting. What makes it moving is that Eowyn's and Merry's courage and defiance are driven by, yea, are made possible by, their *love* for the old king, not a literal father to either but a father figure to both.

"King's man! King's man!"

"I will smite you if you touch him."[126]

Yes.

The tide of battle turns against the West again, only to be reversed once more by Aragorn's force emerging from the Corsairs of Umbar (Can we say, "interlacement"?). And then nothing less than a long lay in alliterative meter could end this chapter. Meanwhile, dark things are happening back in the city and we have no leisure to catch our breath quite yet. Better turn the next page.

---

[126] Ibid., 127.

# DAY 59

# The Return of the King

## *"The Pyre of Denethor"*

"The Pyre of Denethor" is as intense as it gets. If we were wondering what could possibly match the intensity of the battle of the Pelennor, this is it. Everyone is frantic with the imperative necessity to act yet deeply conflicted about the actions required of them. Rushing back to stop the tragedy above, Gandalf knows that others are going to die below because of it. Beregond has to leave his post and break the law of the Citadel to save his Captain—he must violate his oath in order to fulfill it. Blood is shed in the hallows. We are reminded of Dido's suicide in *The Aeneid*, but there are no sword thrusts (*"sic … sic …"*—those percussive monosyllables pounding out from the rolling flow of Virgil's classical hexameter) to bring closure; rather we are left with the image of burning hands forever imprinted on the Palantir, not to mention the minds of everyone present. Wow!

It is all there to drive home the message: "Work of the Enemy!" said Gandalf. "Such deeds he loves, friend at war with friend; loyalty divided in confusion of hearts."[127] The value and the beauty of friendship is one of Tolkien's major themes, as we have seen. It is not just the positive portraits which carry the theme. Enemies like

---

[127] Ibid., 139.

Saruman are incapable of appreciating friendship, and the Enemy passionately hates it. The sowing of discord is not just an instrumental strategy, but something Sauron loves for its own sake.

"Authority is not given you, Steward of Gondor, to choose the hour of your death."[128] Gandalf rebukes Denethor's stubborn insistence on having his own way. If he cannot have victory on his own terms, he will have nothing. That is the place to which Denethor's despair has taken him: suicide on his own terms is preferable even to an honorable defeat. "To me it would not seem that a Steward who faithfully surrenders his charge is diminished in love or honor," Gandalf replies. "And at least you shall not rob your son of his choice while his death is still in doubt."[129] Gandalf achieves victory because he is willing to face defeat, even to choose it over dishonor. This willingness—which is one way of expressing the risk that is inherent in trusting Iluvatar even when you must do so against the temporary testimony of sight—is actually a prerequisite to victory. It does not guarantee victory, but its absence guarantees defeat. Such trust is essential to faithfulness. But that is no longer a choice that Denethor can understand.

And finally, do not trust in your own wisdom to read what the Palantir can show you as if that is more important than trust in Iluvatar. Trust in one's own wisdom flows from the same character flaw as loving too well the work of one's own hands. This last is only implied, not stated; but perhaps that makes it the strongest statement of all.

---

[128] Ibid., 141.
[129] Ibid., 143.

# The Return of the King

### "The Houses of Healing," "The Last Debate," and "The Black Gate Opens"

We need "The Houses of Healing" after "The Pyre of Denethor" almost as much as the characters do. "The hands of the king are the hands of a healer," says Ioreth, "and so shall the rightful king be known."[130] To call Aragorn a Christ-Figure is to say too much, but to miss the fact that he is meant to remind us of Christ the King (as Gandalf reminds us of Christ the Prophet and Frodo Christ the sacrificial Priest) is to say too little. Ioreth's prophecy makes that point hard to miss.

Another of the many reasons we value the work is the vision it gives us of what Pippin calls "the heights" and how they are related to the familiar and homely. "We Tooks and Brandybucks, we can't live long on the heights," Pippin observes. Merry replies,

"No, I can't. Not yet at any rate. But at least, Pippin, we can now see them, and honor them. It is best to love what you are fitted to love, I suppose; you must start somewhere, and have some roots, and the soil of the Shire is deep. Still there are things deeper and higher, and not a gaffer could tend his garden in what he calls

---

[130] Ibid., 150.

peace but for them, whether he knows about them or not. I am glad that I know about them a little."[131]

And I say: This is you and I as we read *The Lord of the Rings*.

"The Last Debate" summarizes the sacrifices all must make for the sake of Frodo's, for without the heroism of each character Frodo and Sam could never have fulfilled their quest. Each one has a different role to play (even Gollum!), and each one is essential. We must keep Sauron's Eye fixed away from his real danger even if it kills us, even if it means we never live to see the new age our sacrifice is making possible. And make no mistake. We are prepared to die for the mere possibility of a new age, not the assurance of it, just because it is the right thing to do. Talk about heights!

And so we arrive at the desolation and the Black Gate. My first time there, I was as despairing as Pippin at the presentation of Frodo's mail and Sam's sword, missing the strange incompleteness of that ensemble. Gandalf did not miss it, and I caught up to him my second time there. It was plain that Mordor had the equipment but not the hobbits. We may still be about to die horribly, but all hope is not yet lost. And so Pippin's consciousness flits away to leave us in the last and worst cliffhanger of all. Tomorrow: Back to Frodo and Sam as the interlacement finally comes to rest, and then on eventually to one of the strangest, most unexpected, but best prepared and most satisfying climaxes in all of literature.

There may come a day when we are dependent on the lame alterations to the story made by Peter Jackson. But it is not this day. This day, we *read*!

---

[131] Ibid., 161.

# DAY 61

# The Return of the King

*"The Tower of Cirith Ingol" and*
*"The Land of Shadow"*

Our first chapter back in Mordor needs to be intense to pull us away from the desperation we just lived through before the Morannon, and it is. Sam does not actually have to do much fighting to rescue Frodo from Cirith Ungol, but he still has to find the courage to attack an installation that should have been manned by several hundred orcs. His song of defiance on the edge of despair is one of high points of the whole trilogy.

> Though here at journey's end I lie
>    In darkness buried deep,
> Beyond all towers strong and high,
>    Beyond all mountains steep,
> Above all shadows rides the sun
>    And stars forever dwell.
> I will not say the day is done
>    Or bid the stars farewell![132]

I have memorized that stanza. You should too. All of us are going to have days when we will need it.

---

[132] Ibid., 204–5

Sam's defiance is rewarded later by a renewal of hope, in another passage that deserves full quotation:

> There, peeping through the cloud-wrack above a dark tor high up in the mountains, Sam saw a star twinkle for a while. The beauty of it smote his heart as he looked up out of the forsaken land, and hope returned to him. For, like a shaft clear and cold, the thought pierced him that in the end the Shadow was only a small and passing thing; there was light and high beauty forever beyond its reach.[133]

What is true on a literal, physical plane reflects what is true in the world of the spirit. Sauron's pitiful fumes and reeks can never rise above the atmosphere to blot out or even threaten the light of the stars. Sam has intuited the truth that Augustine of Hippo would formulate with clarity in a later age: Evil is of necessity a privation of Being, a parasite on the Good. It cannot be otherwise. Unless the Good is logically and ontologically prior, there is nothing there for Evil to pervert, corrupt, or destroy. This does not guarantee that Frodo and Sam will reach the Chamber, much less be able to destroy the Ring. But it does what it needs to do: It renews Sam's hope for one more step.

---

[133] Ibid., 220.

# DAY 62

# The Return of the King

## *"Mount Doom"*

Peter Jackson had to make changes to the story to make it work as a movie instead of as a book: scenes missing, characters conflated, things simplified. That in itself should not be an issue. Unfortunately, some of those changes betrayed a fundamental misunderstanding of the story he was trying to tell and were not just a matter of adaptation but of deformation.

The unrecognizable versions of characters like Faramir and Denethor, having Arwen head off to the Havens, having Frodo tell Sam to go home: these stand out as among the worst changes.[134] But to me the most egregious of all is what might seem to many a subtle addition that makes little difference. It happens in Sammath Naur. In the book, Gollum makes a fatal misstep during his victory dance after biting off Frodo's ring finger and falls into the fire seemingly on his own. In the film, Jackson seems to have Gollum fall over the edge of the crevasse as the result of his struggle with Frodo.

What's the big deal? Isn't Jackson just trying to make the scene more dramatic? No doubt. But in doing so he fundamentally alters a scene Tolkien had spent two and a half volumes setting up and obscures mightily the point that Tolkien's climax carries.

---

[134] For a discussion of why these changes were made in terms of contrasting philosophies of life and of literature, see my chapter "'You're not Telling it Right': Peter Jackson's Betrayal of J. R. R. Tolkien's Vision" in *An Encouraging Thought*, op. cit., 76–89.

Gandalf tells Frodo that Bilbo was *meant* to find the Ring, and not by its maker. This is an encouraging thought because it means that things don't just depend on Gandalf's wisdom and Bilbo's famous luck. Someone else (we know from *The Silmarillion* it is Iluvatar) is at work behind the scenes, and that is the only thing that can make Gandalf's plan real wisdom instead of a fool's hope. And Gollum has a role to play in that for good or ill. So Frodo's ultimate inability to let go of the Ring is overcome by Providential forces *over which he has no control.*

Frodo's faithfulness matters: It gets him to the place where something else that was more than what he had in himself could take over. And that is why Gollum needs to fall by chance (if chance you call it). Every time luck or chance in the whole story is given with one hand to be taken back by the other in those terms, it is working to set this scene up. Jackson undoes what may be the most carefully prepared moment in literature and obscures the theme of Providence Tolkien had worked so hard to weave into the plot, all for the sake of a little extra action.

In his letters, Tolkien calls what happened to Frodo at Sammath Naur "a grace."[135] It is a theological word that is chosen advisedly. Frodo (and through him Middle-earth) is given a *gift*. What he could not have done, being finally worn down by the struggle, is done anyway. What Gollum intends as betrayal becomes the "salvation" (another word used in the same epistolary discussion) of Frodo and of Middle-earth. This is the ultimate fruition of the encouraging thought, a Gift as ironic and eucatastrophic as any ever imagined outside the Gospel itself. It needs to be received, not grabbed, stumbled into, not snatched, found, not seized.

Let Gollum fall as he is fated to!

---

[135] *Letters*, op. cit., 234.

# The Return of the King
## *"The Field of Cormallen" and "The Steward and the King"*

I can think of no other book that goes on as long after its climax as *The Lord of the Rings*—and it is not a word too much. When we finally do reach the end, we are glad we still have the appendices to further delay the inevitable parting.

The celebration of victory at the Field of Cormallen makes Sam wonder if everything sad is going to come untrue. It won't, not within the circles of the world, but we are given a foretaste that justifies the question when the minstrel sings of "Frodo of the Nine Fingers and the Ring of Doom."[136] We join Sam in bursting into tears that are the very wine of blessedness.

Catching up on what happened while he was in Mordor, Sam tries to assimilate "Orcs and talking trees and leagues of grass and galloping riders and glittering caves and white towers and golden halls and tall ships sailing."[137] And this one-sentence summary of what we have all just been through strangely leaves us equally enchanted if not equally bewildered.

It is a great victory and a completely appropriate celebration. But it does not have the eschatological finality we might be

---

[136] ROTK, op. cit., 258.
[137] Ibid., 260.

tempted to give it. Legolas is there with his Elvish perspective on time to bring us back to earth. Evil is defeated but not finally destroyed. We still live in Arda marred, and the Final Chord of the Great Music is not yet, foreshadowed and anticipated though it well may have just been. This respite is real, but it is only a respite; this is the truth implied by Legolas's perspective. The blessing is real, and it will last ... "a month, a life, a hundred years of Men."[138] A passing moment in the life of an Elf, in other words: for his immortality in the life of the world impresses on him at the outset what mortal Men will realize equally at the end: that Time is fleeting. And so Legolas's thoughts even at this moment of triumph turn to the Sea.[139]

Meanwhile, we flash back to Minas Tirith for the love story of Faramir and Eowyn. There is always something new to discover even after more than fifty readings. I cannot believe I waited until this time to notice that Faramir, like Tolkien, had lost his mother as a young lad and to ponder what arraying Eowyn in her mantle must have meant to him and to his creator. We don't need any extra reasons to have an emotional reaction to Tolkien's tale, but they are lurking there just the same. And then, finally, Aragorn and Arwen together at last—but after that comes many partings. It is the way of things in Middle-earth. Shakespeare said it well: "This thou perceivest, that makes thy love more strong / To love that well which thou must leave e'er long."[140]

---

[138] Ibid., 264.

[139] For a full treatment of time, eternity, and eschatology in Middle-earth, see my chapter, "A Far Green Country: The Eschatology of Tolkien's Middle-earth." In *Theology and Tolkien: Constructive Theology*, op. cit., 301–315.

[140] Sonnet 73.

## DAY 64
# The Return of the King
### *"Many Partings"*

"Many Partings" is a chapter that is necessary to the trilogy's ability to mirror real life. Nothing in life is better than our fellowships where friends have each other's backs and work together for a common goal that means something to them, growing close and committed to one another in the process. My high-school band; my college band; the core group from the church I planted in Toccoa in the 1990s; my students who gathered weekly at my house for "Inklings II": Time moves on and the members inevitably scatter. To see one of them again lifts the spirit, but we knew when he said it that Gimli was right because we have seen it in our own stories: "We will send word when we may, and some of us may meet again at times; but I fear that we will not all be gathered together ever again."[141]

There are indeed many partings here. None is more touching than Merry's farewell to Theoden. None is more grievous than Arwen's to Elrond. In casting her lot with Aragorn, she gives up her Elvish immortality within the life of the world for the Gift of Men: a mortal life to which attaches only the vague hope of something that is "more than memory" to be enjoyed "beyond

---

[141] ROTK, op, cit., 289.

the circles of the world."[142] This means that she and her father now have divergent destinies: They no longer share the same afterlife. Elves go to the Halls of Mandos, and what happens to the souls of mortal men is not very well defined in their phase of pre-Biblical revelation. There is no assurance that they will ever meet again, and if they do, it will be in a time and place "beyond the ends of the world."[143]

Arwen and Elrond then represent the theme of great gain only after unspeakable loss that we saw with the Ents and the Entwives on a level perhaps matched only by Frodo. Arwen gains Aragorn, the love of her life, and a new destiny which at the end of her life she is not quite able to appreciate. She also gains the opportunity to bequeath her place on the Ship to Frodo, who will need it. What does Elrond gain other than the satisfaction of knowing he has made a noble sacrifice essential to the proper unfolding of the future of Middle-earth, the sacrifice that Eru Iluvatar has apparently providentially asked of him? If the worth of such gains is incalculable, so is the cost and the loss. At least Tolkien's Elrond does make the sacrifice freely and nobly rather than trying to finagle and manipulate his way out of it, as Peter Jackson's does, actually sending Arwen off to the Grey Havens. And it is no less a sacrifice and no less costly for that!

It is all a foreshadowing of the last meeting on the shores of Middle-earth that is coming at the Havens. And what Gandalf says then we will say now because when we get to that chapter it will bear repeating. "I will not say, do not weep, for not all tears are an evil."[144]

---

[142] Ibid., 389.
[143] Ibid., 285.
[144] Ibid., 347.

# DAY 65

# The Return of the King

## *"Homeward Bound" and "The Scouring of the Shire"*

"Homeward Bound" is a transitional chapter. It's nice to visit The Prancing Pony again and to get Bill the Pony (the eponymous inspiration for this book!) back, and we really wonder what Gandalf and Bombadil are going to talk about, given that Tom won't be very much interested in anything we've just read about except the Ents. Do he and Treebeard have a running argument over who is really the oldest? Probably not. And who is Tom anyway? Nobody has ever caught him; he's the master of water, wood, and hill—we know, we know. Yet we don't know. And I doubt we are ever going to find out.

We are going to find out what's happened to the Shire. It has become the last showpiece for Saruman's malice and bitterness and a profound warning and object lesson about what happens when people are naïve about politicians grasping for power and not vigilant about protecting their rights. My readers will no doubt be divided about which set of our current politicians they think it is warning us against, and I will let them argue that question out among themselves. (My own opinions on the matter are well known and on record elsewhere, and they include the observation that right now both groups might not be wholly wrong.) It is a legitimate question, but a question of what Tolkien called "application,"[145] which lies in the freedom of the reader. Here I want to talk about the *story*.

Tolkien had serious artistic and philosophical reasons for including "The Scouring of the Shire," but he also had an amazing amount of fun with it. Rosie and Sam getting their romance re-started are deliciously awkward at first and then psychologically realistic and emotionally heartening all the way through. Gaffer Gamgee grousing about Sam "wearing ironmongery"[146] still elicits hoots after a half century of reading. Merry and Pippin routing the ruffians is as rousing as any of the great battles that were harder fought with more at stake. I think it is because the evil we are dealing with here hits closer to home in ways we can relate to. How so? Well, we all wish Merry and Pippin could have visited our old grammar-school playgrounds when we think about certain bullies who were wont to lurk there, do we not? And what fun it would have been to have been there then!

Finally, Saruman's end is as fitting as it is unexpected. The rejecting wind that blows out of the West to reduce his shadow to nothingness and consign him to the Void with Melkor and Sauron has a finality to it that shows us why moral choices matter. They are more than just getting correct answers on an ethics quiz. They combine that with issues of loyalty or disloyalty to a Source of the Good who is very personal. Life in Middle-earth has as its purpose making a Decision about that loyalty that will rule your destiny, and there comes a point at which it can no longer be unmade. And so that cold and inexorable wind that comes blowing out of the West has the finality of the New-Testament parable: "And the door was shut" (Matt 25.10).

---

[145] FOTR, op. cit., 11.
[146] ROTK, op. cit., 327.

# DAY 66

# The Return of the King

## *"The Grey Havens"*

From my very first reading to this last one, I have never wanted the book to end. After devouring every word of the appendices in the summer of 1968, I went straight back to volume one and started over. But all temporal things must come to an end, and there are other books that deserve to be read too (if not over fifty times).

Frodo has saved the Shire (not to mention the rest of Middle-earth), but he is too deeply wounded to enjoy it as everyone had hoped he would, and he must eventually leave to find in the West the healing that Arwen had promised when she gave him her place on the Ship.[147] There are those who think Tolkien intolerably cruel to his hero.[148] But though Frodo suffers, he is philosophical rather than bitter about it. "It must often be so, Sam, when things are in danger; someone has to give them up, lose them, so that others may keep them."[149] He does not regret or question the value of his sacrifice any more than he hides what a sacrifice it was. Arwen has promised that he could find "complete healing" in the West if he needed it.[150] And Tolkien himself com-

---

[147] Ibid., 282.
[148] E,g, Verlyn Flieger, "The Arch and the Keystone." *Mythlore* 38:1 (Fall/Winter 2019): 13.
[149] ROTK, op. cit., 345.
[150] Ibid., 382.

mented on Frodo's time in Aman thus: "He went both to a purgatory and a reward, for a while: a period of reflection and peace and a gaining of truer understanding of his position in littleness and in greatness, spent still in Time and the natural beauty of 'Arda unmarred,' the earth unspoiled by evil."[151] So let us say that Tolkien does not minimize the cost of Frodo's sacrifice but gives us a basis for believing that it was worth it, even to Frodo.

If *The Lord of the Rings* does have to end, it is hard to imagine how it could have ended better. As Tolkien has been doing since page one, he makes fantasy the ultimate portrait of real life. For the sad truth about life for mortal men in a fallen world is that things do come to an end and therefore loss is inevitable. But the redeeming fact about it is that even loss can be enriching.

Can there be a greater irony? But so it is for Frodo, who must lose the Shire to gain healing, for the Elves, who must lose Middle-earth to gain the glory of Aman, and for Sam, Merry, and Pippin, who lose Frodo but gain lives of rich memory and great accomplishment because of what they had shared. Gandalf as usual has the best commentary. "Well, here at last, dear friends, on the shores of the sea, comes the end of our fellowship in Middle-earth. Go in peace! I will not say: do not weep, for not all tears are an evil."[152]

Finally, Sam captures perfectly the fact that life goes on, and it will be good both because of and despite the loss (and because of Rosie). "Well, I'm back," he said.[153]

---

[151] *Letters*, 328.
[152] ROTK, op. cit., 346–7.
[153] Ibid., 357.

# DAY 67

# The Return of the King
## *"The Appendices"*

The appendices at the back of *The Return of the King* are a wonderful addition, and the true mark of a Tolkien fan is to think so. They alleviate the gut-wrenching desire to put off ending one's sojourn in Middle-earth; they allow for as much or as little geeking-out as the reader may require; and they contain information that, especially before the publication of *The Silmarillion*, and in some cases even afterward, allows for deeper insight into the meaning and the "applicability" of the larger tale. The information about the Shire calendar and the "Tale of Years" satisfy the first of those desires. The introductions to the languages satisfy the second. (How many of us as teenagers wrote letters to our best friends in English transliterated into Elf Runes?) My main interest at this point lies in the third, which is richly satisfied by "The Tale of Aragorn and Arwen."

In "The Tale of Aragorn and Arwen," we not only find out about their life together in the Fourth Age; we also get one of Tolkien's most profound meditations on what it means to live a life of faith in realities that go beyond what the eye can see. Aragorn grounds his faithfulness to Iluvatar and to his own mission in something larger than the provincial little slice of time available to the direct vision of even a long-lived mortal like himself. Trying to explain to Arwen his costly faithfulness at the end of his life, he roots their lives in more than just the present moment. "Let us not be overthrown at the final test, who of old renounced the Shadow and the Ring. In sorrow we must go, but not in despair. Behold! We are not bound forever to the circles of the world, and beyond them is more than memory. Farewell!"[154] Arwen has given up the immortality of the Elves *within* the circles of the world for her marriage to Aragorn and now finds the Doom of Men hard to bear. Aragorn asks her to find a new hope by looking outside those circles.

What does he mean? He is certainly rejecting the lie that Morgoth told Hurin: "Beyond the Circles of the World there is nothing."[155] Metaphysically, beyond the circles of the world lie two realms we know of: the void into which Morgoth was thrust and the realm of Iluvatar. Temporally, the circles of the world imply the cycles of finite time as mortals know it, beyond which is the Final Chord which renders those cycles linear and thus includes the hope of a meaningful future existence for the Children of Iluvatar. There are no details—only hints—"more than memory"—but that is all Aragorn needs. As with Faramir, Aragorn gives us an eschatological vision in which the meaning of Time is found in its relation to Eternity, and this relationship is one we can trust to be the source of ultimate goodness for us because of the eternal character of Iluvatar.

---

[154] Ibid., 389.
[155] J. R. R. Tolkien, *Unfinished Tales*, op. cit., 67.

# DAY 68a
# "On Fairie Stories"
## *Sub-Creation*

Eventually, even the Appendices are finished, and one has to return to the primary world. But all is not lost. You can proceed to track down, find, and read every other word that your new favorite author has published. That is a daunting and, for many, an impossible task today, thanks to the faithful editorial labors of Tolkien's son Christopher. But back in 1968, the year I found myself in that position, there was an appalling lack of other material. But there was an edited volume called *The Tolkien Reader*, and it had tantalizing offerings including Tolkien's most important non-fiction composition: the essay "On Fairie Stories."

This essay is Tolkien's main contribution to what today we would call "literary theory." It contains two key ideas central to his approach to reading literature and to writing it: the doctrine of sub-creation and the experience of eucatastrophe. Both speak of the centrality of Tolkien's Christian faith to his philosophy of literature and of life, and each deserves a chapter of its own.

Sub-creation is about our very identity as human beings; it applies not just to fairy stories but to all the arts, fine and practical. Human beings are creative because they are made in the image of the Creator. Tolkien sums it up in one sentence: "We make still by the law in which we're made."[156] I can still remember the excitement with which I first read those words as a young high-school student wrestling with whether I could still believe the Christian faith in which I had been reared, given the failure (actually, to be more honest, refusal) of the Christians I knew to interact intelligently and responsibly with the problems of modern thought. For Tolkien had just roped all the problems and their answers together in a single sentence. Man, in other words, is inexplicable by materialist reductionism because of an explicitly Christian doctrine: the *Imago Dei*. We love to tell and hear stories because we are made in the image of the Creator whose creation is in fact the Story we call History and Redemption.

What does this mean? The human race and human beings are incapable of being fully explained by philosophical or portrayed by literary naturalism. We are such irrepressible inventors of things and expressers of ourselves because we are made in the image of the Creator. Hence our outlandish notions like inalienable rights and our addiction to ideals like Goodness, Truth, and Beauty, which refuse to be treated as mere subjective constructs no matter how hard our secular philosophies push us to do so, precisely because it *is* self-evident that we were created, and created by this very specific God.

Out of all the creative possibilities entailed in sub-creation, Tolkien focuses on stories. He builds on the theology of literature found in Sidney's "Defense of Poesy,"[157] expanding it to meet modern questions and providing it with a critical vocabulary. Every writer, like God, creates a world, determines the laws of its nature, and peoples it with characters whose significant actions give that world its meaning. God's "primary world" is reflected

---

[156] Tolkien, "On Fairie Stories," op. cit., 54.

[157] Sir Philip Sidney, "The Defense of Poesy," 1595, *The Renaissance in England: Non-Dramatic Prose and Verse of the Sixteenth Century*, ed. Hyder E. Rollins and Herschel Baker (Lexington, MA: D. C. Heath & Co., 1954): 605–24.

in our "secondary worlds," which, far from being mere escape or wish fulfillment, reflect back into the primary world the marvelous quality—the "enchantment"—that is really there by virtue of its created, its non-reductionist character, but which familiarity and secularist philosophy work to obscure.[158]

In short: If you want to ponder the roots and branches of Tolkien's having planted the world-tree of Middle-earth in rich Christian soil, this is the place to do it.

---

[158] For more on the implications of Tolkien's idea, see my book *Mere Humanity: G. K. Chesterton, C. S. Lewis, and J. R. R. Tolkien on the Human Condition*, 2nd ed. (Tampa: DeWard, 2018), esp. pp. 55–64 and 127–45.

# DAY 68b
# "On Fairie Stories"
## *Eucatastrophe*

One feature of the Faerie Story which is central to Tolkien's literary apologetic is the Happy Ending. It is, he concludes, essential to the form, which begins "Once upon a time" and ends "happily ever after." But it is not just the fact that things turn out well: "It is a sudden and miraculous grace ... It does not deny the existence of ... sorrow and failure: the possibility of these is necessary to the joy of deliverance.[159]" That is why, when the "turn" comes, there is "a catch of the breath, a beat and lifting of the heart ... as keen as that given by any form of literary art."[160] To this moment he gives the technical name *eucatastrophe*.

Tolkien suggests that this moment of *eucatastrophe* in a well-constructed fairy story moves us so because it carries a glimpse of deeper realities about who we are—about our own story. As he explained to his son Christopher, "it produces its peculiar effect because it is a sudden glimpse of Truth; your whole nature chained in material cause and effect, the chain of death, feels a sudden relief as if a major limb out of joint had suddenly snapped back."[161] (If there is a Creator, His Story is the Father of

---

[159] Tolkien, "Fairie Stories," op. cit., 68.

[160] Ibid., 69.

[161] Tolkien, *Letters*, op. cit., 100.

all stories--which is to say that there *is* one valid Metanarrative, and Post-Modernists would not even have the ability to deny it if it did not exist.) And Tolkien is not reticent about spelling out the theological meaning of the climax of our larger story:

> God redeemed the corrupt making creatures, men, in a way fitting to this aspect, as to others, of their strange nature. The Gospels contain a fairy-story, or a story of a larger kind which embraces the essence of fairy-stories.... . Among the marvels is the greatest and most complete conceivable *eucatastrophe*. But this story has entered History and the primary world.[162]

Or, in other words, "Man the story-teller would have to be redeemed in a manner consonant with his nature: by a moving story" which was also history and reality.[163] The incarnation, sacrifice, and resurrection of Christ not only complete and fulfill Old-Testament prophecy, they complete and fulfill the plots of all the great myths and fairy stories of the human race; they are the ultimate eucatastrophe of history.

So the Death and Resurrection of Christ is the fulfillment of much more than just Old-Testament prophecy. All the hints in our literature that we are more than mere collocations of atoms coalesce into a coherent explanation of who and what we are when we see that this *eucatastrophe* is indeed the Happy Ending we were made for: fairy stories do capture something essential to a full view of Reality. As Chesterton put it, "Fairyland is nothing but the sunny country of common sense."[164]

We were made for a higher bliss, and we show it by our own making. We make because we were made in the image of the Maker. What we make is sometimes corrupted because we fell

[162] Tolkien, "Fairie Stories," op. cit., 71.
[163] *Letters*, op. cit., 110.
[164] G. K. Chesterton, *Orthodoxy* (1908; Garden City, NY: Image Books, 1959): 49.

from His grace. But the stories we make as we strut and fret our hour upon the stage still speak of our longing for restoration, because we were made in the image of the Maker who is Savior and Redeemer as well. Christ is what we have always been looking for. He is the ultimate definition of true humanity. So the one vantage point from which our whole strange history makes sense is also the one place where Myth and History are one: the spot where, in the light of the rising sun, the shadow of a Cross points to the open door of an Empty Tomb.[165]

---

[165] To compare C. S. Lewis's way of making this "narrative argument" for Christianity, see his essay "Myth Become Fact," in *God in the Dock: Essays on Theology and Ethics*, ed. Walter Hooper (Grand Rapids: Eerdmans, 1970)" 63–87, and my book *Answers from Aslan: The Enduring Apologetics of C. S. Lewis* (Tampa: DeWard, 2023): 124–37.

# DAY 69
# "Beowulf: The Monsters and the Critics"

Tolkien's reputation as a literary scholar would be assured by this one essay had he done nothing else. It is considered to be a watershed that marks the beginning of the modern literary study of the *Beowulf*, and it is still essential reading for students of the work ninety years after its first appearance—something that is true of *very* few works of literary criticism. Informed readers of it today will see many reasons why it fully deserves that honor. But it is of interest to us in this book primarily for one section: the Allegory of the Tower.

Wait; the *what* of the Tower?

Yes, I typed that word correctly. And yes, Tolkien did tell us in the foreword to *The Fellowship of the Ring* that he "cordially disliked" allegory "in all its manifestations" and had always done so since he was "old and wary enough to detect its presence."[166] So why is there an allegory at the heart of Tolkien's essay, and why is the short story "Leaf by Niggle" quite possible the most intricate allegory since C. S. Lewis's *Pilgrim's Regress*? Because, while Tolkien was surely an honest man, he was also, like Gandalf, capable of blowing smoke on occasion.

Tolkien was perfectly capable, that is, of making strong, dramatic, even iconoclastic statements for their effect at the moment

---

[166] FOTR, op. cit., 10.

without worrying about their consistency with everything else he had said and done. Nobody who truly and literally hated allegory could have written "Leaf by Niggle." What Tolkien hated was people making lame allegorical interpretations of his Trilogy and presenting them as its actual meaning rather than as the reader's (legitimate, by Tolkien's own admission) *application* of a story coming to them not as allegory but as feigned history.[167] I think he probably also hated the fact that so many people use the word *allegory* loosely to refer to any type of symbolism rather than the very specific kind of symbolism it is: symbolism that sets up *systematic* parallelism, like *The Divine Comedy* or *Pilgrim's Progress*, not like *The Lord of the Rings* or even Narnia.

So allegory does have a legitimate place in Tolkien's mind and in his writing. This one makes an important point about his approach to stories. An ancient man built a tower. His friends and his descendants notice that it was built using stones that had previously been parts of other structures and quarried in interesting places. So they push the tower over to study to study them and learn all sorts of interesting things by doing so—except why he had built a silly tower in the first place. But—what they never discover—from the top of that tower the man had been able to look out upon the sea.

The tower is the *Beowulf.* The stones are its sources and the remnants of old lore and old myths that are preserved in it. The point is the limits of form criticism and the necessity of attending to the story *as a story* interpreted in the light of the whole vision that the author had created. It became impossible ever after to go back to the old antiquarian approach to that poem as being, by itself, adequate for understanding the work. And the lesson about how we should read Tolkien's legendarium hardly needs to be stated.

---

[167] Ibid.

# "Smith of Wooton Major"

"Smith of Wooton Major" is such a blessed and priceless little gem that one fears that any commentary would profane it. I shall tread lightly, therefore, with my shoes cast off from my feet, as if on holy ground. I would have saved it for the end if "Leaf by Niggle" did not have an even greater claim to be the last word. It is here because one wants the essays, especially "On Fairie Stories," to be fresh in the mind when it is considered. So let us see if we can catch a glimpse of the eucatastrophic Sea that is visible from the top of this Tower.

This is a story about what can happen on the border when Faery impinges on the mundane world. Wooton Major has a special feast in honor of good children every twenty-four years, to which twenty-four children are invited. A special cake is made for this feast, in which various trinkets are hidden for them to find. One of them, one year, is a silver star from Faery. It is unknowingly swallowed by Smith's son. He later disgorges it and unthinkingly claps it to his forehead, where it sticks and becomes a permanent part of his countenance. It is mostly invisible, but light from it shines from his eyes. He becomes the village blacksmith, but with a seemingly magical feel for beauty. The implements he makes are useful but also unusually comely. He takes occasional mysterious journeys, on which he visits the realm of Faery and has experiences of joy and sorrow there that deepen his insights into life and its meaning:

> Some of his briefer visits he spent looking only at one tree or one flower. But on some of the longer journeys he had seen things of both beauty and terror that he could not clearly remember nor report to his friends, though he knew that they dwelt deep in his heart. But some things he did not forget, and they remained in his mind as wonders and mysteries that he often recalled.[168]

Smith returns from these sojourns with a greater appreciation for beauty and a greater capacity for depths of both joy and sorrow which he communicates in some measure to others, especially his own family. But at the climax of the trips he meets the Queen of Faery and realizes that the time has come to pass his gift on. Though fully sensible of the loss, he does so freely. The star goes into the next Great Cake for the next Twenty-Four Feast and comes to an unlikely recipient who immediately starts showing the mystical effects of the gift. Smith cannot return to Faery but lives on with the wisdom he has gained both from the gift and from its loss.

I have not done justice to the story by a long shot, but I have succeeded if I have motivated you to read it (or re-read it). There will be much there, not for me to explain, but for you to ponder. You may think of the glimpses of the high and noble that will enrich Merry's and Pippin's lives even though they cannot live on those heights.[169] You may think of Frodo observing that sometimes people have to lose things so that others can keep them, and ponder the great loss that came with that great gain.[170] You may think of many moments in your own life

[168] J. R. R. Tolkien, *Smith of Wooton Major and Farmer Giles of Ham* (NY: Ballantine, 1969): 26.

[169] ROTK, op. cit., 161.

[170] Ibid., 345.

of which I have no clue. You may think of Tolkien's discussion of eucatastrophe. I am confident that in thinking of all these things in the light of this story, you will be blessed.

# DAY 71
# "Farmer Giles of Ham"

"Farmer Giles of Ham" is Tolkien having fun, and reading it is us sharing that fun with him. One's enjoyment of the fun is enhanced by imagining how the Inklings must have hooted at it when it was read to them, as it surely must have been, having originally been published in 1949. Sadly, there is no surviving record of that having happened, as far as I can tell. But it was read to an undergraduate group at Worcester College in 1938, and Tolkien reported that "I was very much surprised at the result. The audience was apparently not bored—indeed, they were generally convulsed with mirth."[171]

They were likely convulsed by at least four things. One was the plot of the story, in which a shrewd country farmer delivers his village from a giant and a dragon, more by luck and pluck and being at the right place at the right time than by any traditional heroism. (There is a certain reversal of heroic expectations that reminds one of Kenneth Grahame's *The Reluctant Dragon*.[172]) Second is Tolkien's parody of academic prose, presenting this actually rather silly story with a straight face as serious historical and philological medieval scholarship. Only people who have been subjected to pretentious academic prose in the journals can fully

---

[171] Humphrey Carpenter, *Tolkien, op. cit.* 165–6.
[172] Kenneth Grahame, *The Reluctant Dragon*, illustr. Ernest H. Shepard (N.P.: Holiday House, 1938).

appreciate the tongue-in-cheek send-up of the style: "An excuse for presenting a translation of this curious tale out of its very insular Latin into the modern tongue of the United Kingdom may be found in the glimpse it affords of life in a dark period of the history of Britain, not to mention the light it throws on the origin of some difficult place names."[173] This of course refers to a story which is very obviously being told for the sake of the story itself and has nothing to do with any such things.

Third is the cavalcade of classic British understatements. "A man who has a large and imperial dragon grovelling before hm may be excused if he feels somewhat uplifted."[174] Fourth is the sly lack of respect accorded to the pompous and self-important, especially when they are government officials. The king and his knights are by no means as impressive to the reader as they are to themselves. This subtle bursting of bubbles extends, by the way, to people who are impressed by that pomposity, as when the people of the village's gratification by the king's promises is connected with their ignorance of the actual state of the king's exchequer.[175] Of course, any "application" to one's own government or fellow citizens is properly at the freedom of the reader.[176]

There is nothing particularly profound here. There does not always need to be. But if you want to be treated to some innocent chuckles if not "generally convulsed with mirth," this is the place to go.

---

[173] Tolkien, *Smith* etc., op. cit., 65–6.
[174] Ibid., 112.
[175] Ibid., 122.
[176] FOTR, op. cit., 111.

# DAY 72
# "Leaf by Niggle"

"Leaf by Niggle" may be the most personal and poignant piece Tolkien wrote, with the possible exception of the tale of Beren and Luthien.[177] So personal was it that he had to use allegory to create some distance from himself so he could write it. In hindsight, as we read the story today, we cannot help but see Niggle as Tolkien, the Painting as his never-finished legendarium, the lost Tree as a whole as the (as far as he knew) never-published *Silmarillion*, and the surviving Leaf as *The Hobbit* and *The Lord of the Rings*. (And that fits. But in fact, the work Tolkien feared he would not finish as he was writing the story around 1944 was *The Lord of the Rings* itself.[178]) The neighbor, Parish, is probably not a specific person but represents the constant drain of academic duties, wars, and other "interruptions" that interfered with the completion of Tolkien's life work.

Niggle is a painter who is really good at individual leaves. But his *magnum opus* is a grand picture of a full Tree with a Landscape coming into view behind it. He desperately wants to finish it before a long Journey he has to take, but he keeps getting interrupted by life, and particularly by the needs of his lame neighbor, Parish. He catches his death of a cold caught while on an errand

---

[177] See Day 7, above.
[178] See Carpenter, *Tolkien: A Biography*, op, cit., 195–6, 242.

for Parish and finds himself embarked on the Journey. Meanwhile, the canvass of his Tree is used to patch leaky roofs and is ruined, save for one Leaf that survives for a while as a painting in a museum, until the museum is destroyed by fire—and so Niggle's life work is lost and forgotten forever.

Meanwhile, we follow Niggle on his Journey, which, of course, is Death. He ends up for a while in a hospital that seems to stand for Purgatory, until he is released to a Wood that contains his Tree—now finished but with additions and growth still possible—and beyond which are the mountains he had glimpsed behind it. He completes the Tree with the aid of Parish, of all people, and then travels on to the mountains, leaving Parish, who has to wait for his wife, behind, at least for now. The Tree and its Wood, forgotten on earth, become a haven for other travelers, for some of them the best introduction to the beckoning Mountains.

An entire book could be written on the interpretation of this allegory, but I will just highlight a few points here. Protestants do not believe in Purgatory as an actual place or stage of the next life; they think the lifelong process of sanctification is completed immediately on reaching Heaven by the experience of seeing Christ face to face.[179] But they can appreciate a depiction of sanctification which is, to them, chronologically misplaced. In this one. the key element is grace. Niggle's life work is brought to a fruition he could not have imagined, and he can only say, "It's a gift!"[180]

Tolkien was not impressed by *The Great Divorce* when it was read to the Inklings about this time,[181] and his lack of appreciation for Narnia is legendary.[182] As is usual in such cases, there is more to Tolkien's response than meets the eye. One cannot help

---

[179] 1 Corinthians 13.12, 1 John 3.2.
[180] *Tolkien Reader*, op. cit., 104.
[181] *Letters*, op. cit., 71.
[182] Though exaggerated—see *An Encouraging Thought*, op. cit., 112–29.

but think of Lewis's depictions of Heaven from both of those sources when reading Tolkien's here. Niggle sets off to reach "the high passages, and look at a wider sky, and walk ever further and further toward the mountains, always uphill." These are recognizably the same Mountains Lewis showed us in The Great Divorce, to which one can only say: "Further up and further in!"[183]

---

[183] C. S. Lewis, *The Last Battle* (1956; NY: HarperTrophy, 1964): 213f.

# Conclusion

Thanks for hanging out in Middle-earth with me, Gentle Reader. It's getting on toward my sixtieth trip. It's always good to go, and even better when you have good companions for the journey.

I hope my little book has proved to be what Gandalf called Bill the Pony: "a useful companion." Unpacking Bill's saddle bags, we find insights I did not have on my first trip or two, though inarticulate hunches reaching toward some of them were there even then. I expect at times you responded to them with, "Aha! I always thought so!" When I lecture on Tolkien, people often say that and sometimes add, "But I just did not know how to say it." I expect at times you thought, "I had no idea that was there," and I hope you usually added, "But, by gum, it is!" I guarantee that if we come back next year, we will both find something new. After all my visits, that has never failed.

At this point, I feel the need for an impressive conclusion that would put everything we value about Tolkien and his vision into a brilliant epigrammatic nutshell. But Bill is just a humble hobbit-pony after all, so maybe that is asking too much. Let's just take him out to his stall in the shed, then, give him some well-earned mash, and let him rest until our next quest. Mine will be my fifty-ninth. And maybe this is as good a summation as we can make: That is not one too many!

# Annotated Bibliography

Broadhead, Bradley K. "Freedom and Fidelity: Improvisation in the *Ainulindale*." *Theology and Tolkien: Constructive Theology*, ed. Douglas Estes. NY: Lexington Books/Fortress Academic, 2024: 13–31. Excellent study of The Great Music.

Brown, Devin. *The Christian World of* The Hobbit. Nashville: Abingdon, 2012. Spiritual lessons from Middle Earth.

_____. "An Encouraging Thought": The Interplay of Providence and Free Will in Middle-earth." *Theology and Tolkien: Constructive Theology*, ed. Douglas Estes. NY: Lexington Books/Fortress Academic, 2024: 223–37. The role of Providence in Middle-earth.

Caldecott, Stratford. *The Power of the Ring: The Spiritual Vision behind* The Lord of the Rings *and* The Hobbit. NY: Crossroad, 2003. Significant treatment of spiritual issues.

Carpenter, Humphrey. *The Inklings*. Boston: Houghton Mifflin, 1979. Definitive history of Tolkien's circle.

_____. *Tolkien: A Biography*. Boston: Houghton Mifflin, 2007. The standard biography.

Carter, Lin. *Tolkien: A Look Behind* The Lord of the Rings. N.Y.: Ballantine, 1969. Early appreciation.

Chesterton, G. K. *The Everlasting Man*. NY: Dodd, Mead, & Co., 1925. One source for Tolkien's ideas of sub-creation and eucatastrophe.

_____. *Orthodoxy*. 1908. Garden City, NY: Image Books, 1959. Another source for Tolkien's ideas of sub-creation and eucatastrophe.

Croft, Janet Brennan. *War and the Works of J. R. R. Tolkien*. London: Praeger, 2004. Influence of WWI on *The Lord of the Rings*.

Dante Alighiere. *The Divine Comedy 1: Hell*. Trans. Dorothy L. Sayers. NY: Penguin, 1949. Here for Sayers' commentary on Dante and Beatrice.

_____. *Vita Nuova: Italian Text with Facing English Translation*. Trans. Dino S. Cervigni and Edward Vasta. Notre Dame, IN: Univ. of Notre Dame Pr., 1995. I suggest a parallel between Dante's writing the *Comedia* for Beatrice and Tolkien writing "Beren and Luthien."

Dickerson, Matthew. *Following Gandalf: Epic Battles and Moral Victory in* The Lord of the Rings. Grand Rapids: Brazos, 2003. Devastating critique of the charge that Tolkien glorifies war.

_____. *A Hobbit's Journey: Discovering the Enchantment of Tolkien's Middle Earth*. Grand Rapids: Brazos, 2012. Expanded version of *Following Gandalf*.

Duriez, Colin. *The J. R. R. Tolkien Handbook: A Comprehensive Guide to His Life, Writings, and World of Middle Earth*. Grand Rapids: Baker, 1991. Glossary of terms, characters, etc. from Tolkien's work.

Ellwood, Gracia Fay. *Good News from Tolkien's Middle Earth*. Grand Rapids: Eerdmans, 1970. On the Christian elements in *The Lord of the Rings*.

Estes, Douglas, ed. *Theology and Tolkien: Constructive Theology*. NT: Lexington Books/Fortress Academic, 2024. Collection of essays on topics related to Tolkien's theology; includes a contribution by the current author on the eschatology of Middle-earth.

Flieger, Verlyn. "The Arch and the Keystone." *Mythlore* 38:1 (Fall/Winter 2019): 5–17. Sees "contradiction" as the key to understanding Tolkien. Refuted in Williams, "Keystone or Cornerstone," q.v.

_____. *Splintered Light: Logos and Language in Tolkien's World.* Grand Rapids: Eerdmans, 1983. One of Tolkien's most intelligent and profound interpreters.

Foster, Robert. *A Guide to Middle Earth.* N.Y.: Ballantine, 1971. A concordance to *The Lord of the Rings.*

Freeman, Austin M., ed. *Tolkien among the Theologians.* Zurich: Walking Tree Publishers, 2025. Collection of essays on Tolkien as a theologian.

_____. *Tolkien Dogmatics: Theology through Mythology in the Author of Middle-earth.* Bellingham, WA: Lexham Press, 2023. Substantive and careful recent treatment of Tolkien's theology.

Glyer, Diana Pavlac. *Bandersnatch: C. S. Lewis, J. R. R. Tolkien, and the Creative Collaboration of the Inklings.* Illustr. James A. Owen. Kent, Ohio: Black Squirrel Books, 2016. More popular version of the scholarly *Company They Keep.*

_____. *The Company they Keep: C. S. Lewis and J. R. R. Tolkien as Writers in Community.* Kent, Oh.: Kent State Univ. Pr., 2007. Updates and corrects Carpenter's *The Inklings*, studying them especially as a writer's group.

Grahame, Kenneth. *The Reluctant Dragon.* Illustr. Ernest H. Shepard. N.P.: Holiday House, 1938. Parallels to "Farmer Giles of Ham."

Helms, Randall. *Tolkien and the Silmarils.* Boston: Houghton Mifflin, 1981. Early study of *The Silmarillion.*

_____. *Tolkien's World.* Boston: Houghton Mifflin, 1974. Middle Earth in the light of Tolkien's views of fantasy.

Hillegas, Mark R., ed. *Shadows of Imagination: The Fantasies of C. S. Lewis, J. R. R. Tolkien, and Charles Williams.* Carbondale, IL: Southern Illinois Univ. Pr., 1969. Collection of essays by some of the best Inklings scholars of the mid-Twentieth Century.

Hopkins, Gerard Manley. *The Poems of Gerard Manley Hopkins*. Ed. W. H. Gardner and N. H. MacKenzie. London: Oxford Univ. Pr., 1967. Standard source.

Isaacs, Neil D. and Rose A. Zimbardo. *Tolkien and the Critics: Essays on J. R. R. Tolkien's* The Lord of the Rings. Notre Dame: Univ. of Notre Dame Pr., 1968. Earlier version of Zimbardo & Isaacs contains several essays not in the later collection.

Kilby, Clyde S. *Tolkien and* The Silmarillion: *A Glimpse of the Man and his World*. Wheaton: Harold Shaw, 1976. Early and insightful glimpse at *The Silmarillion* by the dean of American Inklings scholars. Kilby spent a summer helping Tolkien get his notes for the book in order.

Kocher, Paul H. *Master of Middle Earth: The Fiction of J. R. R. Tolkien*. Boston: Houghton Mifflin, 1972. One of the first works to take account of the short fiction in relation to the Middle Earth saga.

Kreeft, Peter J. *The Philosophy of Tolkien: The Worldview behind* The Lord of the Rings. San Francisco: Ignatius, 2005. Asks a series of philosophical questions and gives answers with reference to Tolkien's works.

Lewis, C. S. "The Alliterative Meter." *Selected Literary Essys*, ed. Walter Hooper. Cambridge: Cambridge Univ. Pr., 1969: 15–26. Best introduction to the alliterative meter that Tolkien uses as the poetry of the Rohirrim.

——————. *The Four Loves*. NY: Harcourt, Brace, & World, 1960. Lewis on friendship.

——————. *The Great Divorce*. 1946; NY: HarperCollins, 1971. Analog to Tolkien's vision of Heaven in "Leaf by Niggle."

——————. *The Last Battle*. 1956; NY: HarperTrophy, 1964. Analog to Tolkien's vision of Heaven in "Leaf by Niggle."

——————. *Miracles: A Preliminary Study*. NY: MacMillan, 1947. Parallels to Tolkien's views on myth and the Grand Myth (eucatastrophe).

_____. "Myth Become Fact." *God in the Dock: Essays on Theology and Ethics*, ed. Walter Hooper (Grand Rapids: Eerdmans, 1970)" 63–87. Lewis's version of Tolkien's narrative argument for Christianity.

_____. *The Problem of Pain*. NY: MacMillan, 1967. Lewis on the numinous.

_____. *Surprised by Joy: The Shape of my early Life*. NY: Hartcourt, Brace, & World, 1955. Source of Lewis's concept of *Sehnsucht* or "Joy."

Lobdell, Jared. *England and Always: Tolkien's World of the Rings*. Grand Rapids: Eerdmans, 1981. The Ring trilogy as a new mythology for England.

Manlove, Colin. *Christian Fantasy from 1200 to the Present*. Notre Dame, IN: Univ. of Notre Dame Pr., 1992. Tolkien's fantasy as "obliquely Christian."

Markos, Louis. *On the Shoulders of Hobbits: The Road to Virtue with Tolkien and Lewis*. Chicago: Moody, 2012. Spiritual lessons from Narnia and Middle Earth.

Montgomery, John Warwick, ed. *Myth, Allegory, and Gospel: An Interpretation of J. R. R. Tolkien, C. S. Lewis, G. K. Chesterton, and Charles Williams*. Minneapolis: Bethany, 1974. Includes seminal essay by Kilby on "Mythic and Christian Elements in Tolkien."

Noel, Ruth S. *The Languages of Tolkien's Middle Earth*. Boston: Houghton Mifflin, 1974. Good place to start for linguistics.

Noyes, Russell. *English Romantic Poetry and Prose*. NY: Oxford Univ. Pr., 1956. Source of quotations from Wordsworth, Shelley, etc.

Ordway, Holly. *Tolkien's Faith: A Spiritual Biography*. Elk Grove Village, IL: Word on Fire Academic, 2023. Most substantive spiritual biography.

_____. *Tolkien's Modern Reading: Middle-earth Beyond the Middle Ages*. Elk Grove Village, IL: Word on Fire Academic, 2021. On sources and influences.

Orwell, George. *1984*. 1949; NY: New American Library, 1961. The other most devastating moment in literature.

Pope, Alexander. *The Poems of Alexander Pope*, ed. John Butt. New Haven, CT: Yale Univ. Pr., 1963. Standard source.

Purtill, Richard L. *J. R. R. Tolkien: Myth, Morality, and Religion*. San Francisco: Harper and Row, 1985. Good general treatment.

——————. *Lord of Elves and Eldils: Fantasy and Philosophy in C. S. Lewis and J. R. R. Tolkien*. Grand Rapids: Zondervan, 1974. Title is self-explanatory.

Reilly, R. J. *Romantic Religion: A Study of Barfield, Lewis, Williams, and Tolkien*. Athens: Univ. of Georgia Press, 1971. Tries perhaps a bit too hard to see Barfield as the key to the Inklings' work.

Reynolds, Patricia and Glen H. Goodknight, eds., *Proceedings of the J. R. R. Tolkien Centenary Conference, Keble College, Oxford, 1992*. Altadena, CA: The Mythopoeic Pr., 1995. Substantial collection of essays.

Rios, Jeremy M. "A Chance for Metanarrative to Prove its Quality." *Theology and Tolkien: Constructive Theology*, ed. Douglas Estes. NY: Lexington Books/Fortress Academic, 2024: 203–19. Tolkien's metanarrative as a Christian critique of the modern /post-modern world.

Roby, Kinley E. *J. R. R. Tolkien*. Twayne's English Authors Series. Boston: G. K. Hall, 1980. Basic biographical information.

Salu, Mary and Robert T. Farrell, eds. *J. R. R. Tolkien, Scholar and Storyteller: Essays in Memoriam*. Ithaca: Cornell Univ. Pr., 1979. Substantial collection of essays.

Sayers, Dorothy L. *The Mind of the Maker*. San Francisco: Harper & Row, 1941. Parallels to Tolkien's ideas of sub-creation and eucatastrophe.

Scull, Christina, and Wayne G. Hammond. *The J. R. R. Tolkien Companion and Guide*, 2 vols. Boston: Houghton Mifflin, 2006. Massive and magisterial reference work.

Shakespeare, William. *The Complete Pelican Shakespeare.* Ed. Steven Orgel and A. B. Braunmuller. NY: Penguin, 2002. Source of quotations from Shakespeare.

Shippey, T. A. *The Road to Middle Earth: How J. R. R. Tolkien created a new Mythology.* London: Grafton, 1982. Most important single work of Tolkien scholarship, by Tolkien's successor as professor of Anglo-Saxon at Oxford.

_____. *J. R. R. Tolkien: Author of the Century.* Boston: Houghton Mifflin, 2002. Newer work by the dean of Tolkien scholars.

Sidney, Sir Philip. "The Defense of Poesy." 1595. *The Renaissance in England: Non-Dramatic Prose and Verse of the Sixteenth Century*, ed. Hyder E. Rollins and Herschel Baler. Lexington, MA: D. C. Heath & Co., 1954: 605–24. Foundation of Christian literary theory.

Testi, Claudio A. *Pagan Saints in Middle-earth.* Zurich: Walking Tree, 2018, Wrestles with Christian versus pagan interpretations.

Thomas, David. "History's Redemption: Christ-Centered History Elevates Us All." *Touchstone: A Journal of Mere Christianity* 33:4 (July-August 2020): 39–45. Good on Tolkien's Christian view of history.

Tolkien, Christopher, ed. *The History of Middle-earth.* Three vols. London: HarperCollins, 2002. All the back-story you can handle.

Tolkien, J. R. R. "*Beowulf:* The Monsters and the Critics." *An Anthology of Beowulf Criticism.* Ed. Lewis E. Nicholson. Notre Dame, IN: The Univ. Of Notre Dame Pr., 1963: 51–103.

_____. "Farmer Giles of Ham." *The Tolkien Reader.* NY: Ballantine, 1966: 9–79.

_____. *The Fellowship of the Ring.* 1955; N.Y.: Ballantine, 1982.

_____. *The Hobbit.* 1937; N.Y.: Ballantine, 1982.

_____. "Leaf by Niggle." *The Tolkien Reader*. NY: Ballantine, 1966: 85–112.

_____. *The Letters of J. R. R. Tolkien*. Ed. Humphrey Carpenter. Boston: Houghton Mifflin, 1981.

_____. "On Fairie Stories." *The Tolkien Reader*. NY: Ballantine, 1966: 3–84.

_____. *The Return of the King*. 1955; N.Y.: Ballantine, 1983.

_____. *The Silmarillion*. Ed. Christopher Tolkien. Boston: Houghton Mifflin, 1977.

_____. *Sir Gawain and the Green Knight, Pearl, and Sir Orfeo* Translated by J. R. R. Tolkien. Boston, MA: Houghton Mifflin, 1975.

_____. *Smith of Wooton Major and Farmer Giles of Ham*. NY: Ballantine, 1969.

_____. *The Two Towers*. 1954; N.Y.: Ballantine, 1982.

_____. *Unfinished Tales*. Ed. Christopher Tolkien. Boston: Houghton Mifflin, 1980.

Tolkien, J. R. R. and E. V. Gordon, eds. *Sir Gawain and the Green Knight*, 1925; Second edition ed. Norman Davis. Oxford: The Clarendon Press, 1967.

Urang, Gunnar. *Shadows of Heaven: Religion and Fantasy in the Writings of C. S. Lewis, Charles Williams, and J. R. R. Tolkien*. Philadelphia: Pilgrim Press, 1971. Early attempt to critique both the fiction and the ideas it embodies, vitiated by its modernist perspective.

Weaver, Richard M. *Ideas Have Consequences*. Chicago: Univ. of Chicago Pr., 1948. Classic.

Williams, Donald T. *Answers from Aslan: The Enduring Apologetics of C. S. Lewis*. Tampa: DeWard, 2023. On Lewis's version of the narrative argument for Christianity, which he learned from Tolkien.

_____. *An Encouraging Thought: The Christian Worldview in the Writings of J. R. R. Tolkien,* Cambridge, Oh.: Christian Publishing House, 2018. Subtitle is self-explanatory.

_____. "The Everlasting Hobbit: Perspectives on the Human in Tolkien's Mythos," *Global Journal of Classical Theology* (online) 6:3 (July 2008). Adaptation of chapter from *Mere Humanity.*

_____. "A Far Green Country: The Eschatology of Tolkien's Middle-earth." *Theology and Tolkien: Constructive Theology,* ed. Douglas Estes. NY: Lexington Books/Fortress Academic, 2024: 301–15. The Final Chord of the Great Music provides a *telos* for Middle-earth's feigned history that makes its story meaningful and grounds the wisdom of Gandalf.

_____. "Humanity and Faerie: J. R. R. Tolkien and the Place of Narrative in Conceptualizing the Christian Life," *The Journal for the Association of Biblical Counselors,* (online), January 2009. Adaptation of chapter from *Mere Humanity.*

_____. *Inklings of Reality: Essays toward a Christian Philosophy of Letters.* Toccoa Falls, GA: Toccoa Falls College Press, 1996; 2nd ed., revised and expanded, Lynchburg: Lantern Hollow Press, 2012. Tolkien makes a significant appearance in chapters 1 and 2; chapter 8 (in the 2nd ed., chapter 11) is devoted to him.

_____. "'Is Man a Myth?': Mere Christian Perspectives on the Human," *Mythlore* 23:1 (Summer/fall 2000): 4–19. Chesterton, Lewis, and Tolkien on human nature; was expanded later into the book *Mere Humanity.*

_____. "Keystone or Cornerstone? A Rejoinder to Verlyn Flieger on the Alleged 'Conflicting Sides' of Tolkien's Singular Self," *Mythlore* 40:1 (Fall/Winter 2021): 209–225. https://dc.swosu.edu/mythlore/vol40/iss1/ Defense of Tolkien's own view of the Christian significance of *The Lord of the Rings.*

_____."Literature for Wisdom: Donald T. Williams on Reading in the Service of Christian Living," *Touchstone: A Journal of Mere Christianity* 33:4 (July/August 2020): 20–22. The wisdom in Tolkien's writings.

_____. "Lord, Teach Us to Number our Days: The Significance of Tolkien's Elves." *Inklings of Reality: Essays toward a Christian Philosophy of Letters*, 2nd ed. Lynchburg: Lantern Hollow Press, 2012: 217–228. Tolkien's version of *sensucht* as a key to the meaning of the Ring trilogy.

_____. *Mere Humanity: Christian Perspectives on the Human from G. K. Chesterton, C. S. Lewis, and J. R. R. Tolkien.* Nashville: Broadman & Holman, 2006; 2nd ed. Tampa: DeWard, 2018. Expansion of "Is Man a Myth?" (q.v.); Tolkien *et al.* as antidotes to secular reductionism. Explications of "On Fairie Stories" and the legendarium.

_____. Review of Mark Eddy Smith, *Tolkien's Ordinary Virtues: Exploring the Spiritual Themes of* The Lord of the Rings (Intervarsity, 2002) and Matthew Dickerson, *Following Gandalf: Epic Battles and Moral Victory in* The Lord of the Rings (Brazos, 2003), in *Trinity Journal* NS 26:2 (Fall 2005): 352–3. Review of a mediocre book on Tolkien (Smith), and a good one (Dickerson).

_____. Review of Peter Jackson's "Return of the King," *Mythprint: The Monthly Bulletin of the Mythopoeic Society* 41:1 (Jan. 2004): 12–13. Failure of Jackson's movies accurately to reflect Tolkien's vision.

_____. "An Unexpected Meeting" (short story), *The Lamp-Post* 29:1 (Spring 2005, published Spring 2007), 3–7. Lewis and Tolkien come back to check up on Inklings II.

_____. "The World of the Rings: Why Peter Jackson Was Unable to Film Tolkien's Moral Tale," *Touchstone: A Journal of Mere Christianity* 26:6 (Nov.-Dec. 2013): 14–16. Some of the changes

Jackson made to the books explained by divergent views of the nature and purpose of literature.

Wood, Ralph C. *The Gospel According to Tolkien: Visions of the Kingdom in Middle Earth*. Louisville: Westminster John Knox Press, 2003. Good on Tolkien's eschatology (see chp. 5).

Zimbardo, Rose A. and Neil D. Isaacs. *Understanding The Lord of the Rings: The Best of Tolkien Criticism*. Boston: Houghton Mifflin, 2004. Best collection of essays.

# Index

# Also by Donald T. Williams

## Answers from Aslan
*The Enduring Apologetics of C. S. Lewis*

The world has changed radically in the eighty years since C.S. Lewis wrote his major apologetics works. His arguments are still valid, but that validity might not be as obvious as it used to be. It is not enough then for us just to parrot Lewis. We need to understand him so we can emulate him in a way nuanced to be effective with today's audience. We need to learn from Lewis's methods and approach and understand his proper role as a role model: to teach us how to do our own apologetic in our own voice for our own generation. The purpose of this book is to help him do just that.

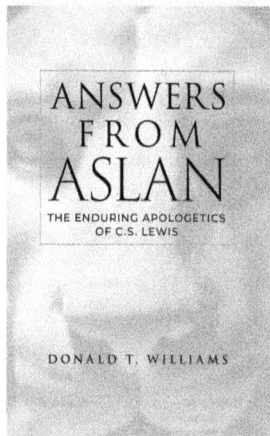

ANSWERS
FROM
ASLAN
THE ENDURING APOLOGETICS
OF C.S. LEWIS

DONALD T. WILLIAMS

# Also by Donald T. Williams

## Mere Humanity
*G.K Chesterton, C.S. Lewis, and J.R.R. Tolkien on the Human Condition*

"Is Man a Myth?" asks the title of one of
Mr. Tumnus's books. It was apparently an
open question in Narnia during the Long
Winter, and it has become so again for us.
In *Mere Humanity*, Donald T. Williams
plumbs the writings of three beloved
Twentieth-Century authors to find
answers that still resonate in the Twen-
ty-First. Chesterton, Lewis, and Tolkien
explain in their expositions and incarnate
in their fiction a robust biblical doctrine
of man that gives us a firm place to stand
against the various forms of reductionism
that dominate our thinking about human
nature today.

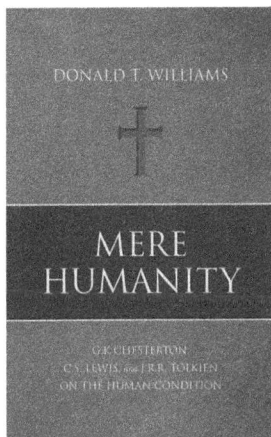

*For a full listing of DeWard Publishing
Company books, visit our website:*

## www.deward.com

DeWard
for your journey

www.ingramcontent.com/pod-product-compliance
Lightning Source LLC
LaVergne TN
LVHW041316080426
835513LV00008B/491